"A really terrific book!

An open time portal revealing historical details, ironic and downright hilarious anecdotes and a political landscape that still resonates today, *Being Fargo* is a must-read, especially for those who already know what it means to *Be Fargo.*

—**Kris Wallman**, State Representative, District 11, Fargo

"... made me laugh and reflect . . . yup, it was pretty much that way."

— **Doug Veitch**, USMC and US Army

"These stories brought both tears of joy and real tears. Just like listening to Don in person." —**Bill Petty**, fellow Fargo Central High grad, Spectrum staffer and veteran

"I recommend this accurate historical account, about which **Don, myself and the other characters involved have all** maintained our silence until now, **waiting only for the statute of limitations to expire."**

—**William "Haybale" Flint**, former co-conspirator

BEING
FARGO

A MEMOIR

8/12/15

[signature]

DON HOMUTH

Being Fargo
A Memoir

Copyright © 2014 by Don Homuth

No money or other payment has been received from any person, company or other entity in exchange for any mention or lack thereof in this book.

Edited and published by Marc de Celle.

Photo of author on back cover by Kathy Cegla.

First Edition, First Printing
December 2014

ISBN 978-0-9830928-4-1

To Kathy Cegla, the great love of my life.
For years she's said I should write these
tales down, in the hope that I might
Stop Repeating Them.

CONTENTS

A Voice Appears

Every so often, a unique voice.

In the morning hours of August 28, 2012, I decided to check my stories@howfargo.com email account. It had been a few weeks since I'd checked it – it's the account where people send me their Fargo stories. There were a few waiting to be read. First, a couple of paragraphs about a doctor who, even though the clinic didn't allow him to put his cell number on his business card, often wrote it on the back, telling his patients, "Don't hesitate to call me outside of business hours." Another about a small North Dakota town welcoming people to stay overnight in their homes when there were too many visitors to a funeral to be accommodated in nearby lodging. A third story was about a local church doing a fundraiser that enabled a local refugee from Liberia to bring her children to the U.S.

All wonderful stories of exactly the kind I wanted for the book I was soon to publish, *Close Encounters of the Fargo Kind,* a collection of Prairie Chicken Soup for the Soul kinds of stories from lots of people around here.

Then I read my first email from Don. He explained that he'd won a signed copy of my book *How Fargo of You* for being the first person to register for the 50th annual reunion of his Fargo High graduating class of '62. At the reunion he'd received the book, and later read it on the train back to Oregon, where he now lived. But his email didn't really grab my attention until the second paragraph, where he told me to

> ...google the phrase "square and stationary earth" for a local hook on who I am. That is also a fun story, and has some Being Fargo bits to it as well.

The odd capitalization caught my eye – not just because it was odd, but because "Being Fargo" was on a very short list of possible titles for my next personal memoir about Fargo.

I had told no one. How could he know about it? I mean, "Being Fargo" was very unique phrasing. He'd even known enough to capitalize it!

Then I read the next paragraph of his email:

> My late father was a Salvation Army officer in the early to mid 50s in Fargo. His office was the upper floor of the current citadel at 304 Roberts – I stopped in Friday to look at it for the first time in a Very long time. In 1957, he had me accompany him on a holiday task that I think may have something to do with what you are discussing.

Hmmm. He'd capitalized Very. Right where a more orthodox approach would dictate *italics*. But he made his point crystal clear: it had been a Very long time – not a very long time, and not even a *very* long time, but a Very long time – since he'd been in his Dad's old Salvation Army citadel on Roberts Street.

He closed the email with:

> Being Fargo started well over a half century ago in my life.

Who was this guy, using a unique phrase I'd kept to myself, capitalizing words as the mood fit him?

I decided to immediately open the story he'd attached, *The Least of These*. It was a story he'd written a few years before, to pass on to younger members of his family.

I devoured it, and immediately wrote Don back. In part:

> ...*The Least of These* is the finest piece of writing I've read in quite a while, anywhere. It's certainly the finest writing anyone's sent me about Fargo, and I've received a couple hundred stories.
>
> What a revelation, that Fargo was like that, and your series of revelations in the years that followed. Really brilliant insights, very well written, self- and life-revealing, held tightly by a riveting narrative. Couldn't have enjoyed it more...
>
> ... and I was stunned when I read your phrase *Being Fargo*.
>
> I'd never read that phrase anywhere before — except in my own notes!
>
> About a month ago, perhaps about the time you emailed me or a few days before, I decided the working title for the sequel to my memoir *How Fargo of You* would be:
>
> ### Being Fargo
>
> So when I read you using that phrase, Being capitalized and all, I got chills up the back of my neck. Had to check behind me to make sure Rod Serling wasn't smoking a cigarette and talking into a camera...

That was all the encouragement Don needed. Soon he was writing me stories about his life in Fargo faster than I could read them.

All these stories have Don's unique style, including his unique sense of capitalization – but the capitalization is just one of several dozen moving parts that work together without a hitch. That's the trick. Does it work? Shakespeare and Joyce broke rules, any and all the rules, as they judged fit, so brilliantly as to invariably intensify, rather than dilute or disrupt, their work. On a more human scale, Gertrude Stein refused to use commas, but this stylistic choice added to, rather than detracting from, her unique Voice. And the poet e.e. cummings never capitalized anything – but not just to be cute. Cummings clearly had a certain sensibility in mind and found omitting capitalization an effective way of pursuing and expressing it.

One thing led to another. I offered to edit Don's stories into a volume. You're holding it. A funny, quirky and enlightening blast from a past I knew nothing about, springing from a mind even more unique than the place he's describing. I now know Fargo in a deeper, funnier way, and have found my favorite writer on the subject.

I know you're going to enjoy Don's tales of an earlier Fargo. But that's not the real reason I wanted to help get his stories out into the world. Don's unique voice is exciting – but even that isn't the core reason I wanted to see him in print.

In his *Afterword*, Don speculates on how growing up in Fargo influenced his development. But there's an assumption underlying his whole discussion that he never speculates about, which is that the real point of life is to Do Some Good.

That's Being Fargo.

Marc de Celle
November 23, 2014

PART I

1.

The Least of These

The images and voices in the memories are in soft focus. They have been revisited many times over nearly fifty years. But during the Christmas Season, they always seem more real...

It was 1956 or 1957. It had to be then, because Dad died in 1958. I was then twelve or thirteen – still a boy, not yet a man.

In Fargo, North Dakota, the street was then called Front Street. (It was renamed Main Avenue later.) At the time, the five or six blocks between Broadway and the Red River were a bad place, where parents told us Not To Go. The south side of the street especially was lined with flophouses and old "hotels" in name only. It might have been described as a Skid Row. Maybe it was a slum. But it was surely nothing at all like Home, in any sense of the word.

The buildings were once white sided, but over the years the paint had grayed almost to black, and much of it had weathered off altogether. And that was from the street! From the back, any past presence of paint was long since gone. There were rickety stairways from second floors to the pounded oily dirt where cars were parked and ofttimes just abandoned. The few people who could be seen moved furtively, seldom by day at all. Their clothes were dirty. They smoked a lot. They didn't shave very often. And they smelled.

They were "bums." Whenever we had to ride our bicycles past that area, we got a chill down our backs, and we rode more quickly, avoiding eye contact and Never saying a word to anyone. We were afraid of them, to tell the truth.

Came near to Christmas that year, and I was ready for the usual round of activities appropriate to a Salvation Army kid. For years, I had rung bells by the kettles. When I wasn't doing that, I was selling the "War Cry" – the Salvation Army's magazine from door to door in neighborhoods. When I was doing that, I got to wear an actual Salvation Army hat. At the time, it seemed like sort of an honor.

The ladies at the citadel had, the previous Sunday, put together several hundred small brown paper grocery bags in the basement kitchen. Into each had gone a handful of nuts, a handful of candy, an orange, an apple, a pair of socks, a pair of cotton gloves, and a copy of the "War Cry." They filled all the counter space and all the tables in the kitchen area.

When school let out for vacation, Dad told me that I was going to come with him today, and told me to help him load several dozen of the bags into his black Chevrolet sedan. So we filled the trunk and the back seat and the floor, and he set off. I figured we were going to deliver the bags, but had no idea where.

I was surprised – no, *shocked* is a better word – when Dad drove behind the buildings on Front Street and pulled up and stopped. He then told me that we were going to deliver these bags to the men who lived in the buildings, and I could carry perhaps five on each arm easily. They didn't weigh much.

I didn't know what to say!

Finally, I said, "But DAD! They are BUMS!" I emphasized the word, trying somehow to make Dad see that we had no

4

business at all with these creatures. This was not the sort of place a Good Boy went, and these were certainly not the sort of people to spend any time at all with.

I think Dad sighed. But he sounded stern. "These are Men – and they are alone at Christmas. They have no families or friends, except each other. Today, we are going to give them something, and we're going to smile and talk with them."

"Just say *Hello*, tell them your name, and that you're from the Sally Ann. Remember that – the Sally Ann, and not the Salvation Army. Give them their bag and wish them Merry Christmas. And if they talk to you, spend a few minutes and listen to them."

"I'll be right with you."

I don't mind saying I was scared. My heart was pounding, and I knew full well I did Not want to do any such thing. But it was Dad telling me what to do, so I'd best just do it. And after all, he said he'd be right with me, so it couldn't be That bad, could it?

I loaded up a dozen bags, and followed Dad into the first building.

Once inside, the first big impression was how it Smelled! Really smelled! It was a combination of kerosene space heater, maybe some food, tobacco smoke or spit from chews, body odor, bad breath and maybe here and there the smell of booze. I wasn't sure about the last – I'd not really smelled any at my house, but imagination filled in the details.

The second big impression was how, when my eyes adjusted from the bright white sun on the snow outside to the dim light filtered through the yellowing window blinds, there was almost a complete lack of color. The linoleum on the floors might once have had color, but it had worn long since, and now served mostly just to cover the wood that could be seen here and there peeking through. The furniture was mostly black, the

5

clothes the men wore were gray or black, with an occasional red/black plaid here and there. They wore hats, even indoors. The walls were a colorless beige, probably from long years of tobacco smoke and kerosene fumes.

The lobbies, or parlors or whatever they were held a half dozen chairs in various stages of repair, and maybe a couple of couches in the same condition. They were clustered around a space heater that was too hot when you were close to it, and too cold if you got more than 10-15 feet away. There were buckets to spit in, ashtrays all over the tables and hallways leading away to the rooms where the men slept.

This was Not a good place for a kid to be! I wanted nothing more than out of there. I whispered to Dad that I *really* wanted to leave. He whispered back that I should just go and do as I was instructed, and that everything would be all right.

So I did. I stammered to the first guy, "Hi. I'm Donald, and this is from the Sally Ann. Merry Christmas."

He smiled. All three teeth looked in pretty bad shape, and when he spoke, his words came out sounding funny. "Thank you So Much! And Merry Christmas to you too, young fella!"

This was not what I'd expected at all.

After maybe three or four more performances, it got a lot easier. On going out to the car to reload for the next round, Dad said I should try to get the guys to talk. I asked him how, and he said he didn't really know. He suggested I should ask their names, and where they were from for starters, and let it go on from there.

So I did that next time. After the next guy looked into his bag, and smiled and looked back at me and said "You folks sure know how to make a guy feel good at Christmas," I asked him who he was and where he came from. And he told me. So did the next. And the next. Only one guy didn't, and he just got a funny look on his face and sort of stared out the window and said he didn't really feel like talking just now. But he did thank me and wish me a Merry Christmas even so.

For years, I remembered their names and the stories they told. Now I can't connect the names with the stories or faces. I wish I could, but Time changes memories. Maybe the connection isn't all that important.

There were the usual names – Louis and Eddie. They knew each other from The War. That would be World War One, not Two. They were from someplace Back East, Indiana maybe. There was a Tom, another Eddie, a couple of Joes. I just don't remember them all any more.

I do remember their stories.

They had fought in The War, and had gone to Washington for their bonus. McArthur ran them out of town with the U.S. Army, and they had never forgiven him – even if he did perform well in World War II. They had worked in the factories and lost their jobs in The Depression. They'd ridden the rails, gone to work with the "CCC," the Civilian Conservation Corps. They'd built the dams and the canals and the highways and the public infrastructure during the '30s that gave this nation a fighting chance in World War II. Some of them had served in that war. One guy had an anchor tattooed on his arm, and said he'd had two ships torpedoed out from under him on the North Atlantic, so after the second time he'd moved as far from the ocean as he could, and Fargo seemed like a good place to be.

It wasn't until later that it came clear to me: These guys *built* this nation. They'd fought for it. They'd had the American Dream and lost it when the Depression came. They'd worked the farms and the factories. They'd become the Arsenal of Democracy when they were too old or too infirm to join up. But they'd had some bad luck, or they'd made some bad choices and got into booze. Either they'd left wives and children, or the other way around. Several said they had families somewhere, but

7

they'd lost track over the years. It no longer mattered – they were alone.

We delivered those bags all that day, Dad and I – probably more than 200 of the bags all told. We always got a smile and a thank you. Sometimes the guys laughed at me – a kid with an adult's Salvation Army hat on. Sometimes their eyes lit up with whatever cheer they could muster. I remember a tear or two, blinked away suddenly.

That was all we did that year. There were no big deal Christmas Dinners to report in the newspaper, like there are today. There were no television cameras to report on a one-time act of charity. I wasn't aware of any of the other churches making the same sort of effort. Maybe they did, and I just didn't see it. But I don't think so. It was certainly never mentioned.

"You folks sure know how to make a guy feel good at Christmas!"

It was a handful of candy, a handful of nuts, an orange, an apple, a pair of cotton socks and a pair of cotton gloves and a church magazine. That's all. I've heard that voice every year since, and I'll hear it all my life.

It took years for me to learn that it wasn't what was in the bag at all.

How could I have known then? I was just a kid.

In the Christmas Service at the citadel, Dad did something unusual in his message. There was all the usual stuff about Christmas and the Wise Men and the Angels and the Baby Jesus. But there was something else too – and the memory has stayed with me.

Somehow, Dad worked in the verse about "Inasmuch as ye have done it unto one of the least of these my brethren, ye have done it unto me." The twenty-fifth chapter of Matthew is not one of your usual Christmas chapters, but it seemed to fit that year.

I want to believe that Dad was trying to tell me something important.

It's been fifty years. I'd like to believe I heard the lesson.

2.

The Boy

You remember how little kids don't always hear things the way they get said? Sort of like in the Christmas carol about "round John, virgin..." For several years, I swear I heard it like that, and could never quite figure out why John's virginity should be mentioned at all.

It's funny what sorts of things stick in one's memory. Though some of the events in these vignettes happened nearly six decades ago, nevertheless they have been clear in my memory over that period, and are true without embellishment – to the best of my memory, anyway.

My family emigrated from Canada in 1951 or so. We moved to Owatonna, Minnesota, where my Dad commanded the local Salvation Army citadel and I first attended an American school. After a year there, we moved to Fargo, and lived in a two-story house at 907 Tenth Street North.

That's where these stories begin. My real formative years as a conscious human being began in Fargo, and so these stories are mostly about Fargo, Fargoans and some events that were sometimes hugely funny, sometimes insightful, ofttimes quite strange, and now and again downright sad. The Slings and

Arrows of Outrageous Fortune do land on kids, but mostly, kids never discuss it with adults.

Adults would laugh.   Adults just wouldn't understand. They couldn't.

But kids could and did.

During the '50s, most adults seemed unaware that kids had Inner Thoughts, and while they were busily inculcating Proper Adult Values, the kids – Their kids – were largely just taking it all in, processing it quite separately through entirely different perceptual frameworks, and deciding on their own what it all really meant. The kids just Never told adults and parents about that.   It was none of their business.   That was when kids still lived in a Kid World, not overly influenced by those who were not really part of it.

There's reason to believe that's still happening now. There's no real reason to suggest that adults are yet aware of it, though.

These stories are as they were, adding up to a tale of one kid finding a way to go from childhood to adulthood in Fargo in the '50s and '60s.

It seems to me as though there are threads in life – we follow one for a while, then it either runs out or we drop it. We pick up another and run with that another while, and the process repeats over and over.   Sometimes the threads come back and rejoin, and interact into a fabric of sorts. If one is very lucky, one can be fortunate enough to see that process through to some sort of resolution. The events actually do link across time.

Who knew?

3.

I (Won't!) Pledge Allegiance to the Flag

I wouldn't do it. Period. Simple as that. I wasn't an American and I was NOT going to pledge to a flag I didn't yet think of as my own.

I started third grade at Roosevelt Elementary School, a block down Tenth Street from the house we'd just moved into. I was entirely unaware, at the time, of the Red Scare and the Mandatory Patriotism going on among the adults. Coming in, I remained a somewhat determinedly nationalistic young Canadian.

First day of school, we were told in first period that we had to stand up, put our hands on (or somewhere near) our hearts, and recite the Pledge of Allegiance to the U.S. flag. I was determined, however, Not to say the pledge, required every morning. (This was several years before the Under God language was inserted, and the U.S. flag still had but 48 stars.).

I wouldn't do it. Period. Simple as that. I wasn't an American and I was NOT going to pledge to a flag I didn't yet think of as my own. (Remember – this was 1953-1954 – the dawn of the McCarthy era, when any unwillingness to publicly demonstrate patriotism was looked upon as Communist – or maybe even worse! I had No idea what that word meant, but I'd heard it was bad.)

The teacher tried to reason with me just to keep order – the First and Foremost obligation of an elementary school teacher.

"Just go ahead and say it with everybody else."

"Nope. I won't do it."

"Why not?"

"Because I'm a Canadian, not an American."

Oh – great start that! First day of school, and I'm drawing a line in the sand with the teacher. Oh well – the idea that Patriotism could involve a personal loyalty to a different country from the U.S. was probably unthinkable. But worse, the idea that a Kid could simply refuse to obey the instructions of a teacher….In A Classroom….In Front Of The Other Kids…was downright subversive. Maybe even Communist – whatever that might be.

So…off to see the Principal. That was Vincent Dodge, whose life path and mine were to cross several times over the years, but this was the first.

"He won't say the Pledge. Make him do it."

Vince was somewhat curious about all of that. "Why won't you say the Pledge?"

"Because I'm a Canadian, not an American, and I'm not going to do it!"

Faced with that sort of rebellion, the best Vince could come up with was to have me sent out of the classroom to stand in the hall, so as to spare the other kids the awful sight of someone Not reciting the Pledge in class. I said I would do that, and it all seemed to go OK.

But hey – first day of school in a new school in a new town. Of course my Mom was going to ask how that went. So I told her.

Enter Mom. Most unhappy indeed! From her point of view, being sent into the hall was tantamount to Being Punished, and she was just Not about to put up with that sort of outrage on her kid. So promptly next morning, Mom walked with me the block to the school, and first thing we went in to see the principal. I was standing right there when Mom opened the conversation.

"I understand you are punishing my son for not saying the Pledge," said Mom. "Why is he being punished?"

"Well, he's not Exactly being punished. He just needs to leave the classroom while the other kids recite the Pledge."

"Do you send other kids out of the room as punishment?"

"Yes."

"Why are you punishing Donald for not doing what he shouldn't have to do in the first place?" (I may have inherited my personal streak of bull-headedness, some call it bloody-mindedness, from my mother.)

"Because all the other kids have to recite the Pledge, and if he's not going to do that, he's disruptive."

"Donald – were you saying or doing anything while the other kids were saying the Pledge?"

"No – I was just sitting there."

"Everybody else has to stand," allowed Dodge.

"If Donald stands quietly, would that be OK?"

"I'm not sure. I'll have to check on that," said Dodge.

"Donald – will you stand quietly while everybody says the Pledge?" asked Mom.

"Sure! I just won't say it." Having drawn the line, I was prepared to defend it forever after. There was No power on this earth that was ever going to change my mind, I recall thinking.

I don't know what discussions were held with the school district officials after that. I do know that next day, I stood up with the other kids while they said the Pledge, and then I sat

14

down after the fifteen-second daily exercise and the school day went on as before.

I did learn, years later, that there had been some talk about calling in The Authorities – who that might have been I have no idea – to Look Into This. It seemed ...well.... subversive, somehow. But once everyone learned that my entire family, save for a brother who had been born in Owatonna the year before, were actually Not Americans, apparently they all backed off and just left things ...and me...alone.

I never did say the Pledge in elementary school. Perhaps because I took the words literally, I waited until I became an American to recite that promise. It seemed the only appropriate thing to do. Now when I say the Pledge, it means something more than a ten-second recitation.

4.

Typesmanship

It was wisest Not to demonstrate too much prowess at skills that adults apparently believed were mostly their own.

I can't write.

In third grade I learned that, despite the best efforts of a teacher to teach what was then called Penmanship (now called Cursive, I'm told). The simple fact of the matter is I just don't do it very well.

Mind you – I really liked printing. I got to be really good at that – could print in nice block letters, keep them more or less in a straight line even without the ruled paper that we always used for class exercises. (I liked the Narrow-Ruled white stuff, but in class we always had that Wide-Ruled stuff that was sort of gray and flimsy.).

Starting in fourth grade, we had to graduate from the far more readable printing and go to Writing for assignments. I ended up with all sorts of problems with my indecipherable scratchings. We had to use pencils, and the #2 Eberhard Fabers weren't all that controllable in the first place. The erasers tended to tear through the paper if one attempted a correction. That resulted in smudges, some quite large.

It was frustrating.

It got no better in fifth grade, save that we switched teachers to someone whose own penmanship was really quite amazingly perfect. When she wrote on the chalkboard, the letters and words were completely consistent and legible, always remaining in a perfectly straight line, even without the rule lines on the blackboard over on the side of the classroom. That's where the students were invited – no, directed – to demonstrate their skill at the lessons for all to see.

I had none to demonstrate. My hand just could not do it – not then, not now.

The Writing teacher would have us do these desk drills. We were not to move the pencil with our fingers alone. We were to move our entire forearm resting on the pad between elbow and hand. I recall filling line after line with O's that had to be of a certain slant, and had to be smoothly connected, and the fingers were supposed to remain mostly fixed while the movement took the entire arm.

There were flourishes too – the Q's looked more like a fancy numeral 2. The top loop of the J had to be the same length as the bottom loop, and all the loops top and bottom had to be the same. There was a curlicue on the left side of the T crossing. We copied upper and lower case letters endlessly – lines at a time.

My fingers didn't do that. Or wouldn't. I tried till my hand cramped, and just could Not do it. The girls in class could, as could some of the boys. But I was fully aware that my writing was the worst in the room. The teacher said so – many times.

The whole Writing/Penmanship matter really became critical in fifth grade, when just before Christmas, we were told that henceforth, once we came back in the New Year, no printed submissions would be accepted. Everything had to be Written.

Suddenly assignments took a very long time to complete. I could think faster than I could put those words on paper, and I

17

could print faster than I could write. I was a good speller (always one of the top two in the bi-weekly spelling bees in front of the class). But then and now, it would be difficult to tell for certain if the words were spelled correctly or not. The teacher, being somewhat punctilious about clarity and other virtues, tended to decide they were not.

My grades plummeted. It was no fun at all! My desperation with this got me pretty discouraged. For a kid who mostly liked school, it was pretty bad.

Mom to the rescue!

Mom sent me to typing class over that summer. Since I was already taking piano lessons and showing some minor competence with that, it seemed like the best way to deal with a bad situation.

Interstate Business College (it's gone now) was then located on Roberts Street in Fargo — just around the corner from the old Post Office Building. It had an early morning summer class that began at 7:30 and lasted until 9:00. I believe it met three days a week – Monday, Wednesday and Friday. Yes – they would accept a fifth grader in the morning class. It would be unusual, but they were quite willing to do it.

Swimming lessons for kids my age began at 9:30 or 10:00 at the Island Park swimming pool. So I could get up early, walk to the business college, take the typing class, walk to my swimming lessons and get back home by noon. This is not the most entertaining way for a kid to spend a summer vacation, but the schedule was quite workable and it promised a solution to an otherwise insoluble problem.

The young women in the typing class thought it was rather cute to have a fifth grade boy in the class. I was the only male of any age. (Men/Males didn't type as a rule then. My father did, but probably because his penmanship was as bad as mine, as I later learned.) I was reasonably adept at it – got to the point

18

where I could type maybe 60 words per minute with only a couple of spelling errors. Even the change from visual typing to "touch typing" went well. Once my fingers got used to the patterns, hitting the correct keys became mostly a matter of muscle memory.

It was a smallish bother when the typing instructor would say "You're going to make a good secretary some day," though. Even then, Men did Not become secretaries. It simply wasn't done.

The summer and the class went well. Fargo was then a city of somewhere in the high thirty-thousands, and in many ways it operated like a small town. I played softball, went to the summer recreation program (then called Playtown) held at Roosevelt School (which is where I learned to do a yo-yo, for which I got to be On Television when WDAY featured all the kids from the playground programs in August) and practiced my typing on an Underwood 5 – a venerable machine that Dad had fixed for me to use.

Thus prepared, I returned to school in sixth grade, still at Roosevelt. The pedantic presumption at the time was that students could be given assignments to write as homework, to be turned in a day or two later for grading.

That's where it all went wrong again!

I had to do, if memory serves – and it may not – a book report. I was a really good reader, and thought that book reports were a nice way to share that information with others. I read book reviews in magazines, and so had a nice grasp of what was involved if it was done properly.

My first book report was two pages, using the space-and-a-half setting on the return lever. I recall thinking to myself that This would work out just fine – now that the teacher could read what I'd written, my grades would be better and the rest of the year would work out.

Nope. Disaster, in fact.

In front of the class, she called me up to her desk.

"Who wrote this?"

"I did."

"No – I mean who *typed* this?"

"I did."

"Did your mother type this for you?"

"No – I did."

Down to the principal's office. Vince Dodge and I were becoming more than nodding acquaintances – which is Not something an elementary student would have found a positive thing at the time.

I recall clearly the look on Vince's face when my outraged teacher marched me into his office and said, "Donald is cheating, and I think his parents are helping him."

This was a severe escalation indeed. Being accused of cheating in school was, at least to me, unthinkable. But having My Mom accused of it was quite another matter entirely.

Vince called my Mom, to relay the teacher's accusation. Mom was just outraged!

"Are you accusing *Me* of cheating?"

"Well, no – it's just that Donald showed up with this homework assignment typed and….." Mom cut him off in mid-sentence.

"Test him. Give him a typewriter and let him type." I could hear the phone slam down.

This simple test matter was apparently unthinkable to elementary school personnel at the time. Now it's called "keyboarding" since one seldom sees an actual typewriter any more, but then Typing was considered to be an adult skill apparently.

Vince took me to the school secretary's desk and sat me down, gave me a sheet of paper and told me to type something.

So I did. I recall the secretary smiling rather broadly at the demonstration. I wasn't quite certain why then, and am still not now. I do have my suspicions, though.

Having thus demonstrated my typing skill, the teacher and the school were still left with a problem. None of the other kids could type. If they couldn't, then I shouldn't be allowed to either.

It wasn't the Information that was important – it was the Format.

So I had to go back to Writing – the one skill I had a problem with and never could quite master to the satisfaction of my penmanship teacher. It was still so bad that the sixth grade teacher and I cut a deal:

I could submit the typed assignments provided that I also submitted a written assignment. So I did that. It didn't take much more time, and I doubt the teacher ever really bothered to read the written papers. It was easier for her to read the typed ones that I handed in at the same time. I just dashed off the written part without really giving it a lot of further thought or effort.

It was an interesting lesson. Not certain precisely how to state it, save that for an elementary school kid at the time, it was wisest Not to demonstrate too much prowess at skills that adults apparently believed were mostly their own.

Or something along that line.

5.

Revelation and Epiphany
In Fifth Grade

Revelation (non-religious definition):
a: an act of revealing to view or making known
b: something that is revealed; especially an enlightening or
astonishing disclosure, i.e., "shocking revelations"
c: a pleasant, often enlightening surprise <her singing was a
revelation>

Epiphany (non-religious definition):
a: a usually sudden manifestation or perception of the
essential nature or meaning of something
b: an intuitive grasp of reality through something (as an event)
usually simple and striking
c: an illuminating discovery, realization, or disclosure
<realizing I could get paid for doing something I liked was an
epiphany that changed the course of my life>

For an elementary school kid in school year 1954-1955, there were clearly two major universal presumptions that *always* applied in *every* situation:

The Teacher knows more than you do – about everything.
The Book is always correct about whatever it's discussing.

Teachers, as authority figures, just plain Knew Stuff. That's why They were teachers – they were the font of Knowledge, and they had Authority not only to impart that knowledge to their students, but to give grades, praise and rewards for a student successfully repeating it on demand. A failure to do so would result in a Bad Grade on the report card.

In the unlikely event (kids never heard about it, certainly) that The Teacher might be in doubt, or need to check on a Fact, there was always The Book. The Book compiled Knowledge in written form, possibly lasting forever. The Book was never to be denied because….it was The Book.

I just never quite got the word on that. It may have been attributable to a failure of parenting, but more likely there are just some kids who are prepared to question just about everything. Even teachers. And books.

In fifth grade at Roosevelt School in Fargo, we got a book about American History. It contained all of the usual tales extant at the time – George Washington actually did cut down a cherry tree, and was praised for admitting it. Historians now know that's probably not true – the myth was likely invented by Parson Mason Weems, who included it in a biography he wrote of Washington shortly after George died. But for kids at the time, it was Truth. The Teacher and The Book both said so.

Though the American History book focused primarily on U.S. national history, it was all but impossible to discuss American History without tangentially mentioning that the early explorers also went to Canada, that the French went to Canada before the English did, and that the French and Indian War (where GW his own hallowed and dignified presidential self first was a military figure) spilled over into Canada.

For us in Fargo, Canada wasn't all that far away anyway.

So, for some very brief time, we discussed Canada.

As previously noted, my family had moved from Canada to the U.S. scarcely three years earlier. I still thought of myself as a Canadian, and was often astonished at the ignorance my friends showed about my home and native land.

I recall once where a guy asked me, "Are you from Canada?"

"Yes."

"OK – then talk Canadian."

"OK. What would you like me to say?"

"Whatever you like."

"OK. The sky is blue and it's a nice day."

"That's American! Say something in Canadian!"

I don't clearly recall to this day how that all ended. It never occurred to someone about my age that Canadians also spoke English. (And to be frank about it, probably better English than they did, at the time.) I had (still have to those who can hear it) a Canadian accent. Whenever I say "I'm just oot and aboot the hoose" there are some who can pick it up and identify it. But I digress....

The Teacher – I forget her name but I can still see her face – was lecturing in front of the class as to how Labrador was a "providence" of Canada. She said it with that air of supreme confidence that teachers had – it was Truth, it was Knowledge and it was Correct.

Well, no – it wasn't. I simply knew better. The fact of the matter is that Labrador is a part of Newfoundland, and together they make up the easternmost Canadian "province." Not "providence." As a ten-year-old, Facts loomed large in my world.

Here was a Teacher saying something that was Not Fact.

That was the Revelation. Teachers were Not always correct. I had no idea!

I couldn't grasp that fully. School is important, and things that are Not Fact had no real place in a class full of kids. It was a situation I could simply Not let go uncorrected. So I raised my hand. The teacher called on me.

"It's province – not providence. And Labrador is not a province by itself – it's part of Newfoundland."

Now those two statements are Fact. They are correct. I just knew it.

However – to have a kid correct a teacher was Simply Not Done. It was such an act of *lese majeste* that The Teacher felt compelled to prove me wrong. So she brought out The Book.

The Book said that Labrador was a province. She read it aloud, pointed it out and told me that I was incorrect. So I blurted out:

"The Book is wrong!"

Yes, I said it. Out loud. Right there in front of the teacher, the other kids and God and everybody. You could hear the kids suddenly inhaling, and the immediate silence spoke volumes. I had gone Well beyond reasonable conduct.

It's one thing to correct a teacher, and that's bad enough. It's quite another order of magnitude greater to question The Book. That's beyond the pale, and cause for yet another visit to the principal's office.

"Donald is deliberately interfering with the class, and I want you to call his parents."

Vince Dodge asked me what had happened, and I told him that The Teacher called it a providence, when the right word is

25

province, and that Labrador isn't a province anyway – it's part of Newfoundland.

Vince looked at the teacher, and she held out The Book. Vince pointed out that The Book said Labrador was a province, and that I should overlook the mispronunciation by the teacher.

So I repeated my earlier statement. *"The book is wrong!"*

There was no turning back. I had condemned myself from my own mouth and had drawn the line. Vince had nothing left to do but call Mom. Since we lived less than a block south of the school, Mom was in the office in about five minutes. She was never one not to defend her kids.

So the entire matter was repeated, The Book was shown to her, and Mom said – I am Not making this up – "The book is wrong." Finally – one for my side. Good on ya, Mom!

The matter was finally resolved by going to the Encyclopaedia Britannica – the repository for all correct knowledge. It gave the correct answer – Labrador was Not a province. It was a part of Newfoundland.

More rational folks would have considered the matter settled then and there. Fact trumped Error, the class would be provided the Truth of it, and all would be well.

No – not in 1954. There were larger issues in play.

The unresolved question was, "What do we do now?"

Here was a kid who had the temerity to correct The Teacher, which act would undermine her authority. The kid also claimed that The Book was wrong, and if it could be wrong in one thing, who knows whether it might also be wrong in something else? The entire pedagogic structure of Education As We Knew It would then be in jeopardy.

I couldn't be allowed to return to class the winner. It was, well, simply unthinkable for a kid to trump The Teacher in such a discussion. I couldn't be allowed to say openly that The Book was wrong. Why, it would give kids reason to question school

26

books. That could be even worse – if such a thing were possible – than questioning The Teacher.

I was sent out of Vince's office while the teacher, Vince and my Mom discussed the whole situation. I only caught scraps of the conversation. Vince defended the teacher and the book. Mom defended me and Truth. It was, alas, not close to an even fight.

I was brought back in and told that I could return to class and the teacher would never bring the matter up ever again. We would not attempt to resolve the Providential status of Labrador, and would simply go on to the next chapter. I had to solemnly promise Never to openly correct the teacher ever again over any subject. If I thought she even Might be wrong, I was to discuss it with her after class and not question it during class.

I still recall something that Fess Parker, in his role as Davy Crocket, said about that same time. On the Disney program, he would smile into the camera and say, "Be sure you're right. Then go ahead."

The Epiphany, however, was clear enough:

It Doesn't Matter whether you're right or not. Authority matters more than Truth.

To simultaneously experience both the Revelation and the Epiphany as a ten-year-old was a genuinely significant lesson I've never forgotten – it remains with me to this day.

I'm still grateful for it.

6.

Hi Ho! Hi Ho!

Off to work we go.

In 1955-1956, an allowance of 25 cents per week wasn't all that large, but it wasn't small either. It was enough to maybe buy a candy bar or a pop, now and again. Down at Herb's Grocery in the 700 block on Tenth Street North, the orange pop in the water-filled cooler was a nickel, and a Nut Goodie was still a dime, but it was Much bigger then than it is now.

In exchange, family responsibilities were minimal. Keep the room clean, do some errands now and again and that pretty much covered it. Special requests had to be made personally, and in a tight family budget, the answer was more likely to be No than anything else.

It took considerable effort to save up enough money to buy a plastic model airplane kit – my great passion at the time.

So it came as a Huge surprise when I was offered an actual job, working for the guy who owned the Toy Chest down on Main Avenue just to the west of Broadway. It was...now be ready for this –

Building Model Airplanes!

As close to heaven as an 11-year-old kid could imagine. He'd pay me a Dollar – a whole Dollar – for every kit I built. The idea was to hang them from wires inside the store so customers could see them once they were built. If memory serves, I built something like twenty or twenty-five of them before he ran out of space for more. But there for one summer, I was in Hog Heaven. It introduced me to the idea that Work need not be something all that terrible

Not exactly a long-term career path, but hey – who could ask for more? The models hung there for a couple of years, then disappeared. Art never lasts forever.

Comic books were another passion of mine at the time. I would wander down to Service Drug Store on Broadway on the corner near St. Mary's Cathedral off Sixth Avenue and read them till they threw me out of the place, which usually took fifteen to twenty minutes. The comic books had ads in the back offering ways to make money.

One day, an ad caught my eye. It was the start of Pre-Printed Christmas Cards – first time I'd ever heard of them, and certainly no one we knew actually sent such things. They were Modern! But the ad offered great riches – Make $25, or $50. Maybe even (gasp!) $100 selling Christmas cards with pre-printed family names inside.

What an innovation! And if a person could make even $25, that would be a sum so large as to be nearly unimaginable.

So I sent in the coupon, without telling my Mom. One of the errands I performed for my allowance was getting the mail and bringing it in. In a few weeks, a package showed up with card samples, ordering forms and even a sales spiel which, if properly delivered to prospective customers, was absolutely Certain to result in sales.

Mom never saw the package. I took it to my room and kept it there under some stuff in the closet. Mom had a most regrettable tendency to intrude herself into matters that were not of her concern, and I didn't want to complicate my life any more than it was.

I pored over the package contents for several days. Memorized the script and practiced it several times to get it right. Thoroughly familiarized myself with The Product – how some cards were only plain, while others came with metallic and glittery decorations of one sort or another. (There was a special name for the high-line cards, but I don't remember what it was. At the time, I recall thinking that no sensible person would ever buy the low-cost ones because they looked so... *Plain*, next to the fancy cards.)

Thus armed, I set out to sell cards. The card company suggested that we start with family and friends, but I had no other family in Fargo at the time, and I wasn't about to start right off with friends.

Teachers! That was the ticket! I knew them, they knew me, and so I looked them up in the phone book – it was still summer, school hadn't started yet – and asked if I could come to their homes (Homes! Go to a teacher's home! Gads!) to talk about the cards. Much to my considerable surprise, they all said yes. Most of the teachers at Roosevelt Elementary School lived reasonably close-by on the North Side, so it wasn't that big a deal to take the folder with the samples and go to visit.

Once inside, I dutifully recited the pre-written pitch, and much to my astonishment, pretty much all of them said Yes – they would love to have such cards. All they had to do was fill out the order blank saying how many boxes they wanted of what design. They didn't even have to make a deposit! They would pay when the item was delivered.

Such a deal!

Once I got used to the idea of someone actually buying what I was selling, I started going door to door. The first meeting wasn't to try to make a sale – it was to make an appointment to discuss the cards at some later time. But the pitch was something about how they were surely going to be buying cards before Christmas anyway, so could they spare me a few minutes to discuss something really new and interesting, at not much greater cost than they would pay at Woolworth's.

Figure maybe one in ten agreed. That meant I could get maybe 3-4 appointments just by knocking on 30-40 doors. That was a piece of cake!

I got a whole bunch of orders. I mean a Lot of orders. It's a little hazy now, but it was something like 40 or 50 all told – which for two months' work mostly in August-September wasn't too bad at all.

The order form I had to send back to the company promised delivery, with the bill due On Approval. I had no idea what that was, but I collected the order forms and sent them in and waited. It took about 2-3 weeks or so – sometime in October – for the boxes of cards to show up.

Large boxes. Not huge, but pretty big. A half dozen of them anyway. Inside were the pre-printed cards the people had ordered, and my job was to deliver them and collect the money.

There was also a bill. The card company wanted payment almost immediately. This was somewhat unexpected.

Naturally that couldn't be hidden from Mom. The discussion had Nothing to do with Business – it was all about Why Hadn't I Told Her What I Was Doing, and how if she'd known she would Never have approved of it. Dad wasn't all that impressed either, until...

He figured out how much I was going to make on the deal.

Something right near a hundred dollars. That's $100! A substantial sum of money indeed. At the time, probably a half a month's pay for him. (Salvation Army officers weren't paid a lot.)

31

This was a Kid –a sixth grader – making a Hundred Bucks unknown to his parents. Unheard of! (This is a fine example of the Approach-Avoidance problem in psychology. For a kid to go off and Do something like that without first asking permission was, well – Wrong. On the other hand, there was that money. What to do?)

My parents fronted the money for the bill and paid it reasonably quickly. I delivered the orders over the next couple of weeks. Everybody paid. Everybody liked the cards.

I don't know what happened to the hundred bucks. I certainly never saw it. It was Far too substantial a sum to be left with a kid. It never made it into a Savings Account with my name on it. I didn't notice any additional expenditures on my behalf. I suspect it got somehow sucked into the family budget and was dispersed that way.

The following year, the card company sent a bunch of mail to me asking if I'd like to do it again. My folks forbade it outright. Several years later, I learned that Dad was embarrassed about what had happened, but I wasn't sure why. I'd have thought he'd have been proud, but there may have been some issue with his kid making that much money just by selling cards.

Ah, well – easy come, easy go. Parents controlled things. Nothing a kid could do about it.

7.

"I'm a Yankee Doodle Dandy..."

The local something-or-other of the Daughters of the American Revolution (which by that time had become notorious as simply the DAR, the "little old ladies in tennis shoes" and part and parcel of the Red Scare) called up Mom and asked if she could come to our house for a visit. She made a quite specific request that I was to be present.

I hated that song. Had several reasons for that – I saw the movie and didn't care for the way it was presented. But then, as a kid I never liked musicals generally. They were boring and featured a lot of folks jumping and cavorting around in odd costumes. I think they called that Choreography, and folks took it a lot more seriously than it ever deserved.

But the main reason – the big one – was the sentiment of the lyrics themselves. I didn't know the words Jingoistic or the nationalist form of Chauvinistic, but I do know that all that hollering about how the singer was "born on the Fourth of July" was at best highly unlikely and nothing to brag about anyway.

Besides, I was a Canadian! Not certain quite what that was (or is even now – Canadians tend to be bothered about that a lot), but I was quite certain it meant that I was Not American. So there!

Mom, exerting that special form of child-bothering authority that Moms have (or had, at the time) somehow knew that I disliked the song intensely. But being Mom, and more interested in compliant behavior than self-esteem at the time, would bring out her kids to show off and perform for visiting relatives and friends. That meant singing.

We could all sing reasonably well. Probably picked it up from Mom, who sang a lot around the place. (One of my favorite things is a cassette tape Mom made before she died several years ago, in which she sang a bunch of songs like "The Wild Colonial Boy" and "Abdullah Bulbul Emir" that she sang to us as kids. I still love it.)

But the song I was always told to sing was That song – I'm a Yankee Doodle Dandy....

I was mortified to do it. Early on I tried to protest, but it was of no use. Mom had Authority – even more than Dad. Potential punishment for inappropriate behavior was always more hinted at than explicit, but the consequences of Not doing what Mom told me to do were not something I cared to face.

So, I would sing the damned song. Figured it was just better to do it and get it over with than to spend any more time trying to get out of it.

Mom was aware of my Canadian nationalism, however. I would get teased about it at school by the mouthbreathers in my class. "Hey Canada Boy! Say something in Canadian." And other stupid things I don't quite recall all these years later.

One day I brought home a notice from the school and showed it to Mom. It was an announcement from the Daughters of the American Revolution that toward the end of the year they were going to have all the fifth graders tested on their knowledge of American History. (We had been studying

34

American History that year – the first time it had been formally introduced into the curriculum as a specific subject.)

Part of the deal was several sheets of questions and answers about American History. There were a Thousand of them! From that long list, one hundred would be selected and whoever scored the best in the school would be recognized at the end-of-the-year awards ceremony, and receive a Certificate Suitable for Framing.

Mom, more than I, sensed an opportunity here for me to get a little revenge. She asked (Asked – a new thing!) how much fun it would be if I were to win that contest. I thought about that – it would be a certain comeuppance if a Canadian kid were to win an American History contest. I agreed.

So Mom and I drilled with that Q/A sheet for several weeks. I memorized both the questions and the answers. She first asked them in order, then switched pages, then asked them in random fashion. I got to where I never missed even one.

When the test finally came, it was only the hundred questions, and I wrote a perfect score – 100 out of 100. The awards ceremony in the small gym was OK. We never did frame the certificate. But the next time someone started with that Canadian Kid teasing, I replied that I knew American History better than he did, and as an American kid, that should be... something. Anyway, the teasing stopped. It was worth the effort.

Essentially the same sort of thing occurred later in eighth grade in Ben Franklin Junior High School. We also studied a unit in American History that year. The Q/A sheet had harder questions, but there were still a thousand of them. Mom and I did the same thing, and it worked the same way. I wrote a perfect test, and on Awards Day got another Certificate Suitable for Framing. Which was never framed. No matter. It was a double win, and highly satisfying to me personally, and it gave Mom some bragging rights about her oldest kid.

That would have been sufficient, but it got funnier a couple of weeks after that.

The local something-or-other of the Daughters of the American Revolution (which by that time had become notorious as simply the DAR, the "little old ladies in tennis shoes" and part and parcel of the Red Scare) called up Mom and asked if she could come to our house for a visit. She made a quite specific request that I was to be present. Mom told me I had to clean up and be there for the visit.

At the appointed hour, the woman showed up and was taken to the living room where Mom gave her a cup of tea and the conversation proceeded from there.

"It's just Such a Pleasure for me to come to visit someone who has won the DAR American History award twice. The DAR appreciates that sort of Patriotism."

Turning to me, she said, "Donald – we are Very proud of you, and I want to congratulate you on demonstrating your knowledge of the history of your country."

I was about to answer, but caught the sideways head movement of Mom and the eye expression suggesting I not say much at all. So I said thank you and mumbled something about enjoying the test and let it go at that.

Returning her attention to Mom, the DAR lady then went on. "The DAR likes to recruit people whose family shows such interest in American History and Patriotism. Have you ever, or would you consider joining the DAR?"

This was a new thing to Mom. No – she hadn't considered it. Mom generally didn't join things at all. She was always somewhat embarrassed she'd never gone past eighth grade in school, and in addition to a certain natural shyness, she had enough of her hands full having 5 kids at home. But she was game to go, and in later years she told me she was mostly curious about what might happen next.

"No," said Mom. "No one has ever asked me to do anything like that. What would it involve?"

"Well, really it's quite simple. If you had anyone in your family who fought in the American Revolution, you are automatically qualified to join. If your family came over later, there's another provision that would get you in. Certainly Donald's performance on the two tests would be very much in your favor."

This is the point where I started to catch on. We did indeed have someone in the family that had participated in the American Revolution. It was something that other relatives often discussed with some pride.

But...on the other side!

Back in that period, our family was comprised of Loyalists. We were part of that approximately one-third of the colonists who did Not want to separate from England, and who worked against the colonial forces. When the war was finally over, the family moved to Canada, where it was given a Crown Grant of land near Toronto – land which is still in the family to this very day, in fact. Mom knew this. But at this point, the movement was underway and nothing was going to stop it.

"Oh yes," Mom said. "We do have a family member who fought in the Revolutionary War. His name was Hickey."

That's a fact. Years later someone did a book on the Ingleside Hickeys. My name and two of my brothers' names are in it.

"Wonderful!" said the woman from the DAR, taking several sheets of printed paper out of her briefcase. "Can we fill out this application now?"

Mom was game. Sure – why not? So the DAR lady filled in the application with the appropriate information about the family – names of the parents, names and ages of all the kids. (Not the Place Of Birth, though. That, apparently, was assumed to have been within the borders of the U.S. if someone had managed to get this far into the application process.)

And then... came the part where the DAR lady asked Mom if she knew which unit or group our predecessor had served in. Mom mentioned something – she knew the family history. The DAR lady looked confused.

"That isn't on our list of known American units," she said, with a note of bewilderment in her voice. She was, though she didn't know it, confronting the Unthinkable, and being forced to think about it.

"Oh – that's maybe not surprising," offered Mom. "It was Loyalist. He supported The Crown."

Everything stopped abruptly. The DAR lady opened and closed her mouth several times before saying anything.

Regaining her composure, she finally said, "This is most unusual. I don't think we've ever offered membership to anyone whose family fought against the United States. I'm going to have to check on this with the national headquarters. I'll get back to you."

She never did. Mom chuckled about that for years.

In Canada, there's a group called the United Empire Loyalists. To them, it's important. They have a register of every descendant of the original group, and my two Canadian-born brothers and I are on that list and eligible for full membership. They have a catalog of identifying symbols, and one year Mom bought a UEL jeweled pin that she wore with considerable pride, especially on Dominion Day, July 1. She was also eligible to use the UEL initials on her signature block, and she had them put on all of her bank checks (cheques, to be punctilious about it.) She was adamant – though she was naturalized years later, she was Still a Canadian, and she was Proud of it.

But she wasn't, alas, eligible to join the DAR.

Ah well.

I still won the American History prize both years. That was more than enough for both of us. Mom always enjoyed retelling that story. I lost both certificates in a move some years later. Wish I still had them. And sometimes, I feel like joining the United Empire Loyalists.

But I probably won't.

8.

The Bicycle

I had been pretty much unaware of how Consumerism affected kids.

Like every kid at the time, I wanted a bicycle. A bicycle meant freedom from Staying In The Yard or Not Going Off The Block. There were parks and other exotic places several blocks away. There were friends to visit and ride around with.

One could even Get Out Of Town on a bicycle at the time. (This had to be undertaken with considerable caution lest Mom hear about it and forbid it. Happily it wasn't all that difficult. Thirteenth Street (now University Drive) North went out past the drive-in theater and one could watch airplanes take off and land at Hector Airport, on the side road just right near the Jewish Cemetery and the cemetery where they buried the nuns from the Sacred Heart Academy and local schools out there.

A bicycle was a Good Thing. And I didn't have one.

The family of Philip Rognlie lived in a duplex just a block down Tenth Avenue from mine, and I used to borrow Collin Rognlie's bike now and again if he wasn't using it. (Phil was the Cub Master for the Cub Scout pack at Roosevelt, and his boy Collin and I were friends from school.) I learned to ride on

Collin's bike. That was nice, but I *still* didn't have one of my own.

Sometime about fifth grade, my parents bought me a bicycle. It was red and white, not terribly fancy and when I first saw it I thought This Is Great! I have my Own Bike. I was initially quite proud and couldn't wait to show it to the kids at school.

Previous to this, I had been pretty much unaware of how Consumerism affected kids.

I got it to school, and showed it to some people I knew. The wrong people. The reaction was Just Awful!

"It's a JC Higgins! Nobody likes JC Higgins!"

That brand was sold through Sears. My folks were dedicated Sears customers for many years. I had No idea that there was a hierarchy of bicycles. The older one I'd borrowed from Collin was maybe a Monarch – or something sold through the Gambles store on Broadway. But it was, according to the boys at school, better than a JC Higgins.

I was stunned! I took those kids – who weren't my real friends – so seriously that I was almost ashamed to ride my own bike. That sort of social peer pressure is pretty hard to resist, and I had no defense against it. Frankly, I'd rather have ridden Collin's borrowed bike than my own.

Turns out that Schwinn was the big deal – the Cadillac of bikes. Especially the ones with the full tank, the horn and headlight combination, and best of all had those springs on the fork. And if one had the plastic streamers out of the handlebars, so much the better. The only modification was to put a plastic playing card on one of the side forks with a clothespin so it made a noise that was Something like a motor. A gaggle of a half dozen of those going down the street could be heard two blocks away.

41

A Schwinn was out of the question – might as well have been made of unobtainium.

The next bike down in the pecking order was Columbia. Not quite the panache of a Schwinn, but certainly more acceptable than a mere JC Higgins.

Saving up enough to buy one on my own didn't offer much hope. I had No way of ever amassing that much money, and besides my folks wouldn't let me spend it on a bike anyway. I already had a bike, and that was Good Enough.

What to do?

I stumbled across a deal offered by the Minneapolis Tribune. They offered premiums to kids who could get subscriptions from people to have the paper delivered to them at home. One of the premiums was a bicycle. A Columbia. Not a fancy Columbia, but a Columbia nevertheless. Single speed (3-speeds were exotic at the time; 10-speeds were years away from the consumer market), no hand brake, no tank, no fancy suspension. But it was a Columbia.

To get the bike required something like 50 subscription orders. Most kids never got there – it took too much effort. If they did it at all, they'd get to maybe 4-5 subscriptions and cash them in on one of the lesser premiums instead.

I figured I could sell fifty subscriptions all on my own without telling my folks, cash them in and get a bike I could hold my head up with. Not the fanciest – but at least socially acceptable.

It took 2-3 months, going door to door. I'd get the subscription orders, take them to the Tribune sales office and file them, keeping a running tally. Finally got to 50 and ordered the bike. Still didn't tell my folks.

Picked it up at the sales office and rode it home. Mom wondered where I'd gotten it, and I told her. She asked why I did that, and I told her so Charles, my next youngest brother, could have the JC Higgins. He was old enough to have a bike of his own. (Let me be honest here – there was Nothing particularly generous about my offer, but Mom didn't know that. I didn't want the JC Higgins to be My bike – I wanted it to be His bike. I wanted nothing to do with it. Mom seems to have bought my rationale. Charles got the Higgins and I kept the Columbia.)

Charles was delighted. I was satisfied. That ended the discussion. Kids are not always noble. But then, adults are not always conscious of what goes on in a kid's world.

9.

The '57 Tornado

The last notable thing I saw was one of the two large elm trees in the front yard, just to the right of the front steps looking out, breaking off nearly at the base and toppling toward the street...

It started as a warm morning, and soon turned into a hot day. At 907 Tenth Street North, kids in the neighborhood got together in the morning to do whatever it was we did fifty years ago, but pretty soon we could hear our Moms calling us.

"There's a tornado warning!" said Mom. She had heard it on the WDAY radio weather report. "I want you to stay in the yard."

Staying In The Yard was somewhere between punishment and cold storage. Not much to do in the yard. I went upstairs to read a book and listen to my crystal radio (Boy Scout project), which had a lot of static rather than the usual faint radio broadcasts that could be picked up by positioning the "cat's whisker" on the little crystal. The book was, if memory serves, one of the "Lucky Star" series of science fiction books, written by Isaac Asimov, though under a different name.

(Why do I remember these small things so vividly? Not sure. The only comparable experience that might suggest something is the way I remember some things from Viet Nam. Put simply, for some odd reason many of the details are in sharp focus, even as some of the larger matters are not. A chance of dying focuses perceptions in strange ways. Or maybe things just look different to 13-year-olds than they do to adults.)

As the day droned on – and droned it surely did – it got warmer and muggier. After lunch, I went outside to look at the sky. Though the sun still shone, the western and northern portion of the sky over Fargo looked dark and ominous, with that sick gray-green sheen that indicates a really bad storm is nearby. So I decided to stay outside and just watch.

Inside the house, the big radio – now turned to a higher volume – gave warnings of Possible Tornadoes several times an hour. Whenever one would come on, Mom would tell everyone in the house to Be Quiet! Everyone would, and we'd listen to the latest discussion on the line of strong thunderstorms approaching Fargo from the southwest.

The heightened sense of anxiety probably came from the tornado that had struck, if memory serves, Walcott the previous year or two before. Dad took me out to see that outcome as part of his duties with the Salvation Army disaster relief effort. Dad and I had seen what a tornado could do up close, and it really was frightening.

Only problem was, Dad wasn't home that day. He was out somewhere in North Dakota attending to his "Rural Service" duties with the Salvation Army. Mom was terribly concerned that he wasn't around, and so was going to keep her kids as close as possible.

Then things started to happen quickly. The sky to the north started to swirl as the thunderstorms started to dissipate their energy. The sky to the west and south was simply dark, and I couldn't see it very well from our yard. It was clear, though, that the winds were picking up rapidly, and clouds seemed to be moving toward us from all directions. At least that's the sense I remember now.

Then came The Warning.

"A tornado has been sighted southwest of Fargo, moving toward the northeast. Take shelter immediately!"

Mom yelled at all the kids to get in the house. We all did, and she herded everyone down into the basement to huddle under a rough table made of what seemed like 6 x 6 legs and 4 x 4 top boards. We had discussed this as the place of shelter previously, probably after the earlier tornado, with a warning that if any strong storm came by, this was the place that I should take everyone if Mom or Dad wasn't home.

I, however, held back just a little. The entrance to the basement was near a doorway with a direct line to the front porch, and I wanted to see what was happening outside. For maybe thirty seconds, I looked.

Rain was coming horizontally. The winds were like nothing I had ever seen before. They weren't a constant velocity – they were more like a hammer, blowing in gusts that had their own sound – something between a roar and a wail. Hard to describe. The screens on the front porch were strained to breaking – and some later did. It was hard to see the houses across the street.

The last notable thing I saw was one of the two large elm trees in the front yard, just to the right of the front steps looking out, breaking off nearly at the base and toppling toward the street. Scared the daylights out of me! Which was just as well because that's when I heard Mom yelling, "Donald – you get Down Here Right Now!" I got down there – Right Now!

The six of us crouching under the table were all terrified. Maybe not the baby sister, who was just one year old at the time. But for the four boys and Mom, the whole house was vibrating and the noise from outside was not the "railroad train" sound, but the loud banshee shrieking of the wind.

And then it was simply over.

We waited a while, then went upstairs, wondering if anything would be left. The house was in pretty good shape, with no major damage other than missing some shingles. The tree was partially into Tenth Street, and it blocked traffic for the few vehicles that were trying to move. Mom made us wait until we heard an All Clear siren – at least we thought we heard one, but it may have just been a fire truck – and Mom told me it was OK for me to look around the neighborhood.

The tornado had apparently really hit just a block up the street or so. At Roosevelt School, the brick chimney out back had been knocked down, which collapsed a wall which exposed the swimming pool we'd always heard about, but had never seen. Several of the houses nearby were damaged, and a lot of trees were down. Up on Twelfth Avenue, across from a fraternity house, the duplex where my two friends from Boy Scouts, George and Jim Bakken lived and where I attended Boy Scout patrol meetings, had its entire north side sheared completely off. A few blocks east of there, just past the open field between Ninth and Tenth Streets where we used to fly kites and play softball, the metal-sheathed house where Bonnie Armstrong (her Dad was a doctor, and bought a Corvette in 1953 or 1954) lived was pretty well torn up. Across the street from that, the house where Joyce Reed (of Reed Cleaners) lived had some damage too – though I can't picture it as clearly. The storm had apparently skipped up and down as it slammed into Fargo, and there were spaces where there was barely any significant damage at all between places that were devastated

Later as the day went on, I got out my Boy Scout hatchet and chopped away at some of the downed trees, just to have something useful to do. I doubt I did all that much, but kids generally couldn't do all that much. Anything was better than nothing.

47

We heard on the radio that there were some deaths beyond "The Slough," a neighborhood where the homes were not well constructed, and where, according to local lore, the Poor People lived.

Later that night, Dad made it back, and immediately positioned the Salvation Army canteen truck in the middle of the area out beyond The Slough. I was recruited to help pass out sandwiches and coffee for the rescue workers well into that night. This was my first time responding to a disaster, and the time just seemed to fly by. I recall I was up pretty late.

I do remember the next day that the reported death toll was something like 11, and I can kindasorta remember a picture in the Fargo Forum of a rescue worker carrying the body of a child. It was taken in the dark, and the bodies highlighted in sharp relief against the dark background.

I worked at the canteen for the next several days, and Dad was pretty well exhausted when the unit was moved elsewhere. It took the rest of the summer to clean the neighborhood up. It was always referred to as "The Tornado." We used to take visitors to see where it hit.

We talked about it for years. But for our family, at least, it was simply a precursor, perhaps an omen, of storms to come.

PART II

10.

The Day the World Changed

My two younger brothers and I were just heading downtown to watch a movie. But as we walked by the garage, I noticed a glow...

As a child he'd had rheumatic fever, and suffered febrile seizures for several days before his stepmother relented and agreed he should go to the hospital. That left him with a heart murmur that kept him from enlisting in the Chaplain's Corps of the Canadian Expeditionary Force during World War II. He did try. I recall seeing his rejection letter years ago. The murmur never went away.

In early 1958, he had a pretty severe bout with pneumonia, and was getting ready to do his first trip back into the rural areas he served. As a rule, he'd get up in the morning and leave fairly early. So we all thought he'd left for the day.

It was April, late afternoon, just starting to get dark outside. My two younger brothers and I were just heading downtown to watch a movie. But as we walked by the garage, I noticed a glow from within. I opened the garage door. The car was there. The light inside the car was on, casting the glow. The driver's side door was open, and my dad's legs were sticking out. Dad was on his back under the dashboard with pliers in his hand. He was apparently fixing his car radio – it had stopped working the week earlier – when the Massive Cardiac Arrest, as I heard doctors refer to it later, hit him. He was stone cold dead when I found him. The pliers were still in his hand. It had to be instantaneous. I still recall that image vividly – as one might reasonably expect with such a shock. His was the first dead body I ever saw, but hardly the last.

There was soon a nasty rumor spreading that he had committed suicide. The official report at the time was that the gas tank was full and the car had not been run. There were no fumes in the garage when my brothers and I found him; the car had clearly not been run. The closed garage door was to be expected, it being a brisk Spring morning. He had obviously left it closed it while he worked on his radio.

Nevertheless, I kept running into that rumor for years afterwards, and became quite angry whenever I heard it. But I know what happened, since I was the one who found him.

11.

Mom

Thoreau once noted that many lead "lives of quiet desperation."
As a general statement about the Human Condition, there's a
great deal of truth to that. Most put on a brave and stoic face,
and even their best friends may not know what's really going on
in their own private lives.

Mom wasn't like that.

By any reasonable standard, Mom had a pretty tough life. A
depression-era child in Canada – where the Depression began
earlier, was deeper and arguably lasted longer than in the U.S. –
things got very tough for her very early. Her Dad burned his
lungs out in a sulfite-process Abitibi paper mill in what was then
Ft. William, Ontario. Her family was on public welfare after
that, and in that era such kids were expected to go to work after
eighth grade. Mom was bright enough, and tried to go to high
school, but couldn't afford to buy a lunch, and the meager
sandwich she brought made her embarrassed to remain.

For a while, she built Curtis Helldivers at a Canada Car
factory for thirty-seven cents an hour. At 18, she married her

Sunday School teacher – my Dad – in the Salvation Army. Five kids over the following 12 years, soon followed by a sudden widowhood, leaving her with five kids, no life insurance (Dad had a pre-existing heart condition), two thousand dollars and a 1958 Chevrolet Biscayne.

The church (the Salvation Army is really a church, not a social service agency) not only wouldn't help her, but did its level best to treat her poorly. Within six months, they told her she had to leave the house at 907 Tenth Street North because they were going to need it for Dad's replacement.

Just after Dad died, the church tried to break the family up, with each of us going to separate Salvation Army families to be raised as good little Salvationists. She refused even to discuss it, but the whole experience sent her into a deep depression. She couldn't understand why they were so out to get her. But they were.

She bought her own house – a tad run-down but large enough for the five of us plus her own mother – at 1430 Fifth Avenue South for $10,000 in late 1958. Less than a couple of months later, the church sold our previous house, at 907 Tenth Street North, for less than that, and never did replace Dad.

She hated the Salvation Army thereafter till the day she died.

It's not clear whether it was this experience alone, or the other numerous bitternesses she experienced during her previous young life that caused her to become proficient at Holding A Grudge. She didn't just hold it – she held it close, cherished it, invested in it, got a great deal of interest from it and just generally that became if not The dominant part of her personality, certainly a major one.

I hold no blame to her for that. She had good reason to feel mildly paranoid about some things in her life. There had been people who really Were out to get her.

She became both a fierce and over-protective parent. She was not about to allow her kids to be influenced by "those bastards" out there.

Eventually she would fail in that – and become bitter about that, too.

But perhaps not to the bitter end.

12.

Work as Work

Everything changed, dramatically and suddenly. Work became a necessity, not an optional activity. We moved to the house on Fifth Avenue South, I transferred from Ben Franklin Junior High to Agassiz Junior High. And times got tough! Really tough.

From April 1958 into early 1959, I tried a paper route. I had to walk to the Forum building to get the papers, fold and fill the large over-the-shoulder Fargo Forum bag and walk it back to my neighborhood to deliver them. Sunday mornings were the worst – the papers were heavy, and the Sunday edition ofttimes required two bags, one over each shoulder. In the winter, it was simply unbearable. It was nearly two miles from the Forum to my neighborhood, and I had no one to drive me if conditions were bad. It was walk or nothing, and nothing wasn't an option.

Once we moved to the south side, I couldn't do the walk there, go to the north side and and walk back home again, much less deliver things on time. That effort failed.

Mom had no employable skills. She'd only gone through eighth grade in school and had never worked outside the home. She enrolled in Interstate Business College to get some, and worked part time for Richtmann's Printing on Main Avenue operating a machine to glue NCR receipt papers together. She worked alone, usually at night. I would bike over to bring her some supper and occasionally accompany her home. She couldn't drive, and we didn't have a car, anyway.

In ninth grade, I got a job after school washing windows and mopping floors at Thompson's Women's and Children's Wear on Broadway, right beside the Gambles store at the time. I'd go there after school, and clean the outside of all the windows. Winter or summer didn't matter – the windows were cleaned daily. If it was cold, I'd dump a bottle of alcohol into the soap-and-water mixture.

After the windows were washed, I'd mop the entire floor inside – front to back of the store. Mrs. Thompson wouldn't stand for the sort of wet-mopping that just pushed the dirt around. The floor had to be rinsed with clear water – so two trips through the floor.

Mom got the money for the family budget.

I later added another store – a drug store on Main Avenue just east of Eighth Street that had later closing hours than Thompson's. So I'd hike over there and do their floors on the way home. But that lasted only a few months – it was simply too much time to be spent working, and school started to suffer. I left that job without any regret.

I also did housework. My duties as the eldest kid at home left me knowing how to do housework. For a while, I worked for a family that had a Very large house on several lots on Fifth Avenue and Eleventh Street South. I think the name was Greving. The woman who lived there was getting along, and I did everything she asked, mostly on weekends. Hard work, but she paid promptly and I gave the money to Mom.

It was no big deal – it was just The Thing To Do because that was The Way Things Were at the time. We had to eat.

Later, in high school, I worked as a busboy and dishwasher for The Bowler out on South University Avenue. My girlfriend at the time was a waitress there. Got minimum wage, plus some percentage of tips from the waitresses for doing the table-clearing and setting. The money was OK, but being able to take home the leftover food also helped alleviate some strain on the family budget. The buffet at The Bowler used to have a lot of food left over, so I could take home some pretty good stuff.

Along about 1961 or so, Mom remarried to a very nice man – one of the bravest I've ever met. He married a widow with five kids! That's bravery if I ever saw it. Martin Mickelson owned and operated a small shop in the near north side that made postformed Formica counter tops, and shipped them all over the upper Midwest. He didn't make a lot of money, but it was more than we'd had. Mom ended up keeping the books for the business, and was no longer formally employed by anyone else.

That took most of the financial pressure off. We were by no means well-off, but we were no longer genuinely poor.

(An aside here: Though Mom had been offered "welfare" for her family for some years, her memories of Being On Welfare in her own childhood were both vivid and bitter. She vowed Never to do that, and she never did. Even when things got desperate – and they sometimes were – she maintained that, and never Once considered any other course. Got to admire her for that – and I do.)

13.

Let Us Be Prankful

Little kids can't really do good pranks. There's a good reason for that – if they did Really good ones, they'd get into trouble with adults. Adults don't like it much when kids pull a good prank on them, so kids tend to do Kid Pranks, and be thought of as cute when they do it. But there comes a time when kids get old enough to put together a well-thought-out prank.

The earliest really good prank I recall my friends participating in was at Agassiz Junior High School, in the Spring of ninth grade, when we were getting ready to leave for Fargo Central High. Les Pavek, who later became the Dean of Students at NDSU, was then a gym teacher at the school. He drove a small black Simca Aronde – a little French 4-door that few of us had ever seen before. It wasn't a Folksbuggen. Those were common and scarce worthy of notice in 1959. (Truth of the matter is, there were few VW's around in the first place, but then there were fewer Simcas than that.)

Several of us looked long and hard at the Simca. It seemed that Just Maybe it was about the same length as the distance between two trees on the south lawn of Agassiz. We weren't quite sure, but a tape measure brought to school the next day confirmed it. Same, within maybe two inches. And the length of the car was the shorter of the two distances.

There was the opportunity!

Just suppose you could pick the car up and put it precisely between the two trees. There would be No way to get it out. The trees wouldn't be harmed, the lawn wouldn't be harmed, the car wouldn't be harmed. But the car would just sit there till someone got it out.

Simple yet creative, met all the requirements of a good prank. All it took was about two dozen kids to pick it up and Carry it to the two trees, and put it down Precisely at the midpoint of the front and back bumpers, and voila! (It was a French car, after all) the car would just sit there till someone figured out how to move it. They weren't about to cut down the trees. The idea wasn't to imprison the car for all time – it was just to show that a good prank had been pulled.

Worked like a charm. Les was properly put out, the principal even more so, and in the fullness of time - no more than a couple of hours – the same kids who put it there took it back out and Les drove it home.

Now this prank wasn't particularly subtle, though in retrospect it was still pretty good. No real harm done, no criminal actions. Just creative cleverness properly applied and properly remediated. To my memory it's about the only really good one we pulled at Agassiz, and besides, we were getting ready to go to high school the following Fall anyway. That offered far more potential than junior high ever could.

14.

The Fargo Midgets

"When some loud braggart tries to put me down
And says his school is great
I tell him right away now what's the matter buddy
Ain't you heard of my school
Its number one in the state...."

Oh. Give. Me. A. Break!

Fargo Central High School was the biggest high school in North Dakota. That's pretty much the end of the #1 discussion for any other practical purposes. Because other than that...

We were the Midgets. The flaming Midgets, ferpete'ssakes! Midgets??? Come On Here!

It's unclear to this day whether or not that name was chosen for the sheer irony of it, or whether someone was trying to make a statement of some sort. Whatever it was, FCHS was not the sort of institution fraught with that whole School Spirit thing – or at least not in my memory. The sense of attending it was more one of quiet certainty – we were simply a Really good school during the years 1959 – 1962. We needed not explain it or defend it under any circumstances to anyone else anywhere.

It's been somewhat difficult trying to parse out the several sorts of memories involved in the whole Fargo Central milieu. Each of us experienced our high school years in some wildly different ways. Each of our memory sets is colored by our specific perceptions of what was going on in our own lives, and not across the whole group of students at the time.

For the sake of discussion, I've divided out some – not all – of those memories and perceptions into four broad areas: Athletics, the Building Itself, the Faculty and the Student Body. Those seem sufficient to give a flavor of the experience, without going into a lot of matters further than they reasonably deserve. Each of them didn't affect each of us the same way. But they all affected us.

Athletics

To my memory, not the Midgets' strong suit at the time. The two local television sports directors – Bill Weaver on WDAY and Jim Adelson on KXJB – were somewhat frustrated that the FCHS didn't win many state championships in football, basketball or track. They would, on occasion, wonder why that was so.

There were two reasons:

1. Shanley High School – the Catholic school across town – prided itself on winning a lot of athletic competitions of various sorts. It could, and it did, recruit from the best parochial school athletes in eastern ND and western MN. It made a big deal out of winning, and deservedly so. Shanley also had Sid Cichy, a genuinely competent coach in pretty much any athletic competition of any real importance. He was a dedicated coach and pretty much only interested in his own single school. He was approached with college coaching opportunities many times, and turned them all

down. Just didn't want to do that. As a result, he became a revered figure in local coaching.

2. The thing that never got mentioned much at the time, though, was that FCHS kids just didn't much care about that. It's not clear in my memory whether this was because they simply conceded such things to the Shanley High Deacons, or they were mostly indifferent about such stuff. Perhaps the name – the *Midgets* – made it difficult, in at least a subliminal if not overtly embarrassing way, to get too excited about any athletic competition. At any rate, it just wasn't all that big a deal. There was that group of Team Supporters – the Jocks (and the cheerleaders) who worked at making a big deal out of it, but it was mostly a *pro forma* exercise. I recall attending One football game at the stadium, which was located more than a mile away down on Thirteenth Avenue South. I don't recall ever having attended a basketball game, and the thought of attending a track meet simply didn't cross my awareness threshold. Even at ensuing reunions over the years, the star athletes weren't the ones who got introduced to the attendees. It's simply not as big in our memories as other folks might want to believe.

The Building Itself

Even at the time, I thought the building that housed FCHS was a magnificent and formidable structure. A strange architectural admixture, with early 20th century windows and trim, but nearly medieval crenellations along the "towers" at the top, and the semi-basement first floor had what looked to all the world like a moat standing out from it. It stood on a raised berm, also reminiscent of medieval castles, though more likely merely the wreckage of the previous school, which burned in 1915. The replacement I knew was built in 1920.

The classrooms inside were high-ceilinged and had lots of glass. They were astonishingly light and well-lit – at the time it was built that had to be relatively unusual. Most high schools I've visited that predated Central were notable for being a lot darker. The hallways were wide and lined with lockers. The stairways between the three floors were wide, but even then had to be declared One-Way due to the press of the students moving from class to class.

Everyone seems to remember the creaky wooden floors. In some ways, they were more like a sounding board and gave off loud sounds whenever even a single person walked on them. When everyone was walking between classes, the sound was quite noticeable.

It didn't have a dedicated Gymnasium. There was a large space behind the curtain in the auditorium that served as a gym in the main building.

The auditorium was astonishing. The lowest seats were at the semi-basement level, just below the stage floor, and the highest seats were clear up on the third floor. It had some wonderful acoustic qualities – especially during the music concerts.

It had a swimming pool! Not a big one, but adequate. The boys all skinny-dipped. There was much speculation about whether or not the girls did – at least amongst the boys – but the general consensus was that they did not. Anyone caught doing reconnaissance work to determine the fact of the matter was subject to considerable discipline.

It just had to be a huge energy hog. The windows were all single-pane glass, and were not always well puttied in their casements. Some of the classrooms were drafty – some overly warm.

But it did have a welcoming sense to it, unlike more modern, more efficient schools. There was no efficient movement of students from class to class when the period was over. More like pandemonium, a sort of Chinese Fire Drill. Yet the kids got to where they needed to go.

But by 1960, the science labs and spaces were already dated. Having been built in 1920 to plans earlier than that, the facilities were inadequate for their purposes, so we ended up dealing with crowded labs and some mildly dangerous conditions. But we got through it somehow.

The school burned to the ground on April 19, 1966. My family has an interesting connection to that event and day.

The day was bright and beautiful, as Spring days in Fargo can sometimes be. My brother, Larry, was going into the school that morning, and as countless other students have said about their school over the years, he made a gratuitous comment:

"Gee, what a beautiful day! Wouldn't it be great if the school burned down today?"

And it did!

Of course, several of his compatriots heard him say that, and in the ensuing investigation, he was considered a possible arson suspect for several days. But things worked out – it was discovered the fire had begun above the auditorium in a nearly inaccessible place. So in the fullness of time, he was exonerated entirely.

I actually felt sorry to see it go. I always rather liked the idea of a single campus-style high school, where the kids from all over the city could attend, sufficient faculty and resources could be brought to one place and it would serve to unite, rather than divide, the North and South Sides of Fargo. That was probably a pipe dream, but to my mind, a rather nice one.

The Faculty

If FCHS was blessed with any one singular thing, it had to be the faculty. They were quite astonishingly competent, dedicated, and somehow kept a sense of humor through the performance of their duties that people say is lacking today. That's as it may be now, but it surely wasn't that way then.

The story was that most of the teachers at FCHS had Master's degrees – mostly in the subject they taught, rather than the currently more-often involved advanced degree in Education. As a result, FCHS students could be quite certain that the teachers actually Knew Something – and probably more than even the best of the students did.

Few of the teachers were actually Old – as in the way we perceived many of the other teachers as we came up through elementary and junior high schools. But they weren't just fresh out of university either – most were reasonably mature, had families themselves and were probably in their mid-30s or early 40s.

Did that matter? Yeah – it quite probably did. The old teachers would have predated World War II, and such folks could be and many times were stuck in their old ways. One got the sense that all in all they would have preferred to see the clock turned backwards, to return once again to The Way Things Used To Be – a time when they were more comfortable and assured in their status. They did not care to deal with the sorts of uncertainties that were, even then, starting to be noticeable in so many ways across American society. Fargo may have been a geographical backwater, but it was no longer so entirely cut off from the rest of the world as before.

It was a post-Sputnik era. The Soviets were a clear and present danger. We weren't still doing A-bomb drills as we had been several years earlier, but we were aware that those jet fighters out of Hector Airport from the ND Air National Guard weren't going to stop anything coming at us. The Chinese were still decades away from becoming a genuine international competitor, but the memories of the People's Republic of China's involvement with Korea were very much alive, having occurred scarce ten years earlier.

The faculty at FCHS never perseverated on such matters, but they didn't shy away from mentioning them either. I recall many of the lessons in the Science and Math subjects were considered important for something having to do with those sorts of forces. Even if it wasn't quite perfectly clear why that was so, it was also never all that far out of mind either.

Enough of that.

The biggest thing about those of us fortunate to attend FCHS at the time was that we had it all. This was before the time of Back to the Basics education, huge budget cuts and the like. If it could be offered as a class, it got offered.

Not everyone did, but a good many took full advantage of that. We could take Speech courses, including theatrical studies. There were One-Act play student productions. We could take the full courses in the Sciences – Biology, Chemistry and Physics from the sophomore to the senior year. We had Algebra, Trigonometry, plane and solid geometry. We had great courses in English and Literature – taught by people with a genuine enthusiasm for the subjects. We had excellent History courses.

I simply must mention R.D. Olsen – the World History teacher. The first teacher and one of only a few who could write an entertaining final exam. I recall one instance where as the class was writing the exam in the multiple choice portion, there would be a titter from various students in an otherwise quiet classroom. I don't recall all of it, but among the choices provided were: Themistocles (the correct choice), Douglas MacArthur and the one that caused the laughter – Jubilation T Cornpone. If you don't know why that's funny, look it up.

We had a full house of Music – Band and Orchestra and really good choirs. FCHS did do Very well indeed with some of the regional competitions in music. For example, there were three levels of choir – the regular school choir, the *a capella* choir which was just a small step above, and a very small ensemble group selected from the *a capella* choir which performed very difficult modernistic music.

The same was true of the Bands and the Orchestras. One large group in which pretty much everyone could perform, and a couple of other options for the more musically skilled. Musical Talent was to be admired and encouraged.

We had some Home Economics, metal and wood shops and even the start of a car repair class.

Over on the non-varsity Physical Education side of things, we had intramural activities, from water polo to ping-pong to bowling to archery as after-school activities. There were so many offerings that it would have been all but impossible for any one person to attend as many as s/he might otherwise choose.

It has since become Conventional Wisdom that the proliferation of such Non-Basic education courses detracted from the more general sorts of educational attainment. It did not. Fact of the matter was, given excellent and informed teachers and a panoply of choices of what to study and even from whom, educational attainment in FCHS was pretty high. Turns out that smart and competent teachers resulted in smart, accomplished students.

No school system can do that without an outstanding faculty. We were blessed to have a good one.

The Student Body

It's tempting to go rather deeper into this discussion than is necessary. There's also no real sense to it. As with any reasonably large high school of its time, the student body was diverse and eclectic. But there are some broad strokes that applied then and still seem to apply now.

The student body was anything but monolithic. To describe it properly would require some Venn Diagrams – those intersecting circles that allow structure to reveal itself in some ofttimes unexpected ways.

Economic Class Differences. No question who the Rich Kids were. We all knew them, their parents' names were well-known in Fargo social circles. They moved in their own circles. They didn't have part-time jobs after school. They "went to the lakes" in the summertime. They were the ones that others considered to be Popular – and being popular was considered the highest pinnacle that could be reached.

The kids from Poor Families weren't nearly so noticeable. They were the ones who dropped out. When they left "to go to work" it was still possible to do that sort of thing. They simply disappeared off the map – few remembered them after they'd gone, they didn't show up in the school yearbooks and they didn't attend reunions. They just simply....weren't.

Jocks and Nerds. Not so much of that. Oh yes – there were some Jocks, but it wasn't all that big a deal. If one was Only a jock, it wasn't saying all that much. To this day, I have No idea who the quarterback for the football team was. It simply didn't much matter.

The Nerds tended toward the standoffish sort. There were some Really smart kids in the school, and most folks respected them, even if they didn't socialize with them or frankly like them all that much.

The Music Kids. Smallish group, but we knew who they were. In the great scheme of things, none was destined to become a concert-quality musician, but there was a level of talent that showed.

This was not quite the same as the musically talented kids who played in Rock and Roll bands in the area. We had several of those, and they were quite good. But save for Bobby Vee some years earlier, national recognition and fame (and wealth) would forever remain just out of reach.

Everybody Else. That left everybody else – and within that largest group there was a range of family incomes from Almost Rich to Nearly Poor, but those were the kids who hung in there, went to class and seldom made any waves. They had a job to do – Go To School – and they were about doing that.

There was some movement among groups, but not that much. It was possible, for example, to move downward from the popular/rich group, but all but impossible for anyone to move up into it. One either was a jock or was not. The smart kids simply were who they were – and didn't much care about any of that social stuff.

The Music Kids pretty much started out and remained a static group. One either had the talent (and the lessons) or one did not.

One really didn't socialize much with anyone outside of one's own groups. The rich kids were invited to each others' parties – and nobody else was. The popular songs of the time that occasionally discussed how a rich boy/girl would become romantically involved with someone of a higher/lower socioeconomic class didn't happen. If anything, the girl was the lower status individual striving to move upward, and the relationship tended to be exploitive.

That brief description fails to catch the fullness of the society in FCHS. There were numerous cross- and under-currents of interpersonal relationships, betrayals, new romances, attainments good and bad. It just didn't seem to matter all that

70

much, or at least not that I could tell at the time. Mostly kids just wanted to finish school, go to college and get on with their lives.

Discussions in later years with the faculty indicated that the Class of 1962 stood out for them. We were, so they said, a really good class. Not given to troublemaking, good students, clever in ways that were not mean-spirited (we were great pranksters, as you'll soon learn) and a genuine pleasure to have around.

So, the answer to the question "Where were You in '62?" was obvious. We were in Fargo, North Dakota. It wasn't big, it wasn't small. It wasn't California, but we had heard of that exotic place. It wasn't Peyton Place – even though most of us avidly read the book and even marked the special pages that caused everyone such upset at the time. We had cliques (the girls called them Potlucks, and some of them have survived to this day) but not gangs. Doing violence would have simply been unthinkable, so it mostly didn't happen. It was a time before serious drugs (the Rock and Roll bands were reputed to have some of those, but the regular kids got along on alcohol – considered to be far more benign, even by parents at the time).

In the larger sense, we were Not – by inspection – Baby Boomers. We were born in 1944, when World War II was still raging. The Boomers started to come along a couple of years later. Having one foot in the '40s/'50s looking backward, and another in the then-nascent '60s, we were an In Between group. We weren't quite yet in the Sexual Revolution, but we thought about it a lot and welcomed it when it finally showed up. We predated the political upheavals of the later '60s. In my class, I know of five, including myself, who served in Viet Nam – and one was killed there in 1969.

We did not, by and large, stay in touch all that much over the ensuing decades, although a Central High Alumni Club sprang up a few decades ago and is still, I understand, quite large and holds several luncheons every summer. And oddly,

71

one of my classmates lives not a mile from me today, in Oregon. We played in the orchestra and were each part of the Music Kid group. We accidentally ran across each other at the local university here. We don't socialize. Our lives simply went in different ways, and that's OK. There's another guy who lives maybe fifty miles away. He sends e-mails about every six months saying how he's going to get on his motorcycle and come down. I've told him I'd do a barbeque on the back porch and we'd kick back with a beer and ribs, and remember things.

I've enjoyed the three reunions I've attended. In my mind's eye, I recall those people as they were and I've always been curious about who they became over the ensuing years. By this time, most of the old pretenses have been dropped and we can simply relate as mature adults. I'm struck by how fondly I think of them now, and how gently the old memories come back for review. I'm glad to have known them all, and pleased that at some point we got to share some space and time together on this good Earth and in that good place.

15.

Pranks Be To God

High School was prime time for pranks.

The guy who deserves the praise for the phrase "Pranks Be to God" is the Rev. Dave Knecht, who was at one time the main pastor of the "other Methodist Church" in Fargo – Faith Methodist near North High School.

The occasion was some sort of Legislative Day, sponsored by the Methodist Youth Fellowship chapters from around the state. The participants were bunked at the McCabe Methodist Church, located hard by the State Capitol Building in Bismarck.

Rev. Knecht figured He Was In Charge of keeping all those teenage hormones properly in check, and when it came time to sack out, he made it Quite clear: Boys Will Remain in the room assigned to them. (I suspect no one ever figured the girls would do much of anything, so no warning was necessary.)

Dave got it all wrong. He thought he had Given An Order. Several of us figured it was more like a recommendation, and it was up to us to find a way around it. Which we did. We didn't sneak into the girls' dorm – that was never the point. We just figured to wander around some. In the pews.

Of course we got caught. It was no big deal. But just Think of it – we were chewed out for being "caught" in amongst the pews of the church!

"So what was This all about?" he demanded. "I told you boys Not to leave the room, but you just had to do it, didn't you? Why? What were you doing?"

No one answered. What would he have accepted anyway? But he had to continue with the chewing out....

"I do believe that if you had been with Moses, when the Ten Commandments came down the mountain, you'd have taken them as the Ten Suggestions!!"

We tried not to snicker. Really we did. We failed. Badly.

Dave got disgusted, told us to go back to the room, and walked away.

Perfect!

Dave Knecht made a name for himself as Chaplain to the local North Dakota Air National Guard later on. He never forgot the pranking episode, and reminded me of it for years after.

Pranking on friends

It's pretty much OK to prank your friends, Provided they get a chance to prank you back in turn. Don't prank your enemies. They might hurt you.

I ran with a group of guys who would prank each other mercilessly. And prank their parents, who were mostly good sports, and the worst they ever seem to have gotten was annoyed.

There was the night Jon Houtkooper, Steve Nelson and I picked up some flashing signs from a construction site and put them in the driveway of Bill Flint's house. His Dad, Harold (of the advertising company) woke Bill in the middle of the night and demanded the flashing lights be removed. They were rather like sawhorses, and Bill picked one up by the crosspiece with the light on it. Whereupon one of the side pieces fell in and landed on his foot.

Apparently it is possible to ionize air without the use of electricity – selected language alone can do it. Something about the air turning blue – which has to be an ionic reaction of some sort.

Or the night we filled bill's 1953 Plymouth with three hay bales and cut the strings. Then watched him driving around looking for us on Broadway with hay flying out the windows.

Barry Weingarten was the son of Sam Weingarten, of Weingarten's Clothiers on the corner of Fifth Street and Main Avenue. That family was the target of a really good post-Christmas prank. A bunch of us cruised around town picking up discarded Christmas trees and planted them in the snow in Sam's front yard, with a sign that read "Weingarten's After Christmas Tree Sale." Bless Sam's heart – he put up with a lot. Or maybe he didn't. Barry never really said.

Bill, Jon and Dick Brandon got me back later when I was in college. They put sod completely into the entry and stairs of my apartment, watered it and waited. Got me pretty good!

Fargo Central High School offered a prankster's playing field of considerable opportunity. The juniors and seniors, having driver's licenses and therefore cars, did some things that were mildly reprehensible. Backing up on the sidewalk in front of the school and "peeling out" (also known as "laying rubber") down the sidewalk was always laudable, but it was far too common. Happened several times a year, and a mere replication of other pranks just didn't fulfill the need to pull off some really good ones. Likewise, "cutting donuts" on the front lawn verged over to the vandalism/criminal side of things. That did some actual damage - something that could get a person into trouble and was therefore to be avoided.

75

We were then old enough where that sort of thing actually mattered.

Several other creative pranks high school pranks come to memory:

The brick

The long study hall across from the library was overseen by Miss Pfeffer. She was there to maintain Quiet, and was relatively good at it. Since it was easy enough to spot whoever was whispering or acting up, it wasn't terribly difficult. This was "Honors" study hall – the best students were in it.

One day Sam Brekke brought a brick in his briefcase. It was one of those glazed bricks. At his desk in the back of the room, he took it out and gave it to the person in front of him, and whispered "Pass it on." Now just why that seemed amusing at the time I don't quite remember. It just was.

So the brick got passed to the front of the room, and when Miss Pfeffer wasn't looking, went to the next row over and got passed toward the back with the same suggestion. This went on for a row or two. There was some mild tittering and an occasional outright giggle from those who got it.

Eventually Miss Pfeffer noticed Something Is Going On, intercepted the brick and demanded to know what it was. The individual said s/he (I don't recall exactly which) got it from the person behind, who pointed behind to the next desk and so on till it was traced back to Sam.

"What's this?" asked Miss Pfeffer.

"It's a brick," replied Sam, with a straight face that was in itself hugely humorous to see.

"Why did you bring a brick to study hall?"

"To show it to everybody else."

"Why are you showing it to everybody else?"

"It's a really nice brick."

76

Peals of laughter. Miss Pfeffer confiscated the brick. I don't think Sam ever got it back.

Ball bearing in study hall

Sam again, only this time not with a brick, but instead, a very large ball bearing – about six inches in diameter. Weighed several pounds. I have no idea where he got it. But there was a chance for some creative prankery.

Miss Pfeffer left the room temporarily, Sam hauled the bearing out of his briefcase and rolled it down the row to the front of the room, where it was intercepted and stashed inside a desk. This may seem like no big deal, but you had to know those oak floors of FCHS.

From below, the Sound was apparently quite loud, and sounded as though some serious industrial machinery were being dragged down the row. Within a few minutes, someone from the offices below came into study hall and demanded to know what was going on.

No one said a word. Ever.

BBs rattling down the air shafts

There used to be a little plastic BB shooter you could buy from the back of a comic book that you could load maybe 12-15 BBs into, turn a crank and it would shoot a stream of them. Not enough velocity actually to hurt anyone, but they could go a considerable distance.

So, wait till Miss Pfeffer was out of the room, fire the BBs into the air shaft, where they would rattle loudly down three floors. Right past the Principal's office. Inquiries were made. No one ever said a thing.

Gluing the school shut

One evening, quite late, Sam came to the school and glued every door lock shut. The maintenance personnel arrived early to find themselves locked out. Technicians Were Summoned, and the opening of school was delayed slightly that day. Acetone apparently solved the problem.

I thought this was closer to vandalism than prankage, and I asked Sam why he did it. "Because I could," was his reply. No point taking it any farther.

The choir humming in study hall

Clyde Willman, the principal, and Otto Bernhoft (aka "Big Toot," to differentiate him from his son Frank, a classmate, who was known to some as "Little Toot") finally decided the Honors Study Hall kids were taking advantage of their special treatment. We were to be dispersed into the Big study hall, held in the 3-story school auditorium and overseen by Mr. Pilkey, the boys' gym teacher, who regularly worse muscle shirts to school. Not only were we dispersed, but we were separated by two or three seats from other students. The acoustics of the room were really good – someone whispering in the back rows two floors up from the stage could easily be heard down by the stage.

This constituted A Challenge. Took some pondering, but we worked it out.

Turns out that a good many of the kids were also members of the choirs – and FCHS had Really good choirs at the time. There was room for some truly creative pranking, even with something this unexpected.

The way we worked it out was this:

At some point, the basses from the choir would start to hum a note. It was important not to laugh or smile about it. But it was easy to hear.

The tenors would join in a major third above that, then the altos and then the sopranos a full octave above that. That would constitute a proper chord in four-part harmony. For the choir, it was remarkably easy.

And it worked like a charm first time out. With all the participants keeping a studiously straight face, the chord was launched, and it downright resonated through the auditorium. Obviously Mr. Pilkey had to say something.

"Who's doing that? Stop that right now!"

Well, of Course we weren't about to stop. Way too much potential for that. The chord continued to resonate.

Pilkey then started going up and down the aisles, listening closely for who was doing the humming. No way he was ever going to know – whenever he got close, the individuals simply stopped humming until he went away, then started in again.

A musical prank! Who knew?

We did this again, and the second time Pilkey called Willman in, who demanded that everyone should stop humming. Which, on its own, was amusing too. Despite this success, we only did it one more time, and repeating it wasn't all that satisfying.

Prankery is its own reward, and the creativity involved, as well as knowing we could prank at will, was better than simple repetition.

16.

Sex, Cars and Rock'n'Roll

This discussion usually gets folks my age a little uncomfortable, with downcast eyes and shifting of weight from foot to foot, and a certain reluctance even to acknowledge what we were really like Back Then. Can't really speak for the girls – not being a girl and all. There is reason to believe that the girls at the time were every bit as complicit in the goings-on as were the boys. They just mostly kept quieter about it – though, I learned later, not so much to each other.

Being more or less normal American kids in the late '50s and '60s, we were Nuts about cars, addicted to Rock and Roll, and Horny.

This gave rise to some really quite odd behaviors, and the interface among them could occasionally result in some quite funny and irrational outcomes. It's hard to separate and differentiate them – in some fascinating ways they all sort of ran together. But that shouldn't stop us from remembering...

Cars

In Fargo, there being at the time none of those Wholesome Car Events sponsored by the local police and Chamber of Commerce in the vain hope of Keeping The Kids Off The Streets, the weekend ritual was Dragging Broadway. On a pleasant Friday or Saturday night, pretty much anyone who either had a car or could borrow his folks' (or just flat-out lie to get it, pretending to run some errand or another elsewhere) would find it *de rigueur* at least to make an appearance on Broadway.

In the late '50s Broadway downtown was not really Paved, as the term is correctly used. Instead it was built of bricks, many of which were left over from the Great Fargo Fire of decades earlier, so the story went. Given the nature of the underlying soil along the street, the cold weather, rain and dry weather caused the surface of Broadway to heave and buckle to some quite astonishing degrees.

Frankly, it was downright unsafe to drive on, really. But it was Broadway, so drive on it we could and did. There was nowhere else.

The local big deal car club at the time was the Toppers. You had to have a pretty nice car or know someone in the club in order to be a member. They had really neat little cast pewter Topper signs attached to the rear bumper, so everyone could know who they were. If memory serves, they also had jackets. (Modern historical research on the phenomenon may be done by watching the movie "American Graffiti" in which the Pharaohs also had jackets, and I swear some of the cars in the movie were very like the ones on Broadway at the time.)

One car in particular sticks out – it was a 1949 or 1950 Mercury 2-door post, with frenched-in tail lights from a 1954 Mercury. It was maroon in color, lowered, louvered (Clarence's Louver Shop out on Thirteenth Avenue South) and even had "Lake Pipes" along the side in my mind's eye.

It was magnificent!

It may have been fast. I don't know – few ever did. There's a good reason for that.

81

Due to the heaves in the surface of Broadway, any car with a lowered suspension (and a good many with stock suspensions) just plain couldn't go very fast. One lowered a car by taking a blowtorch to the springs and heating them till they sagged. Looked great, but didn't do much for the springiness of the spring. The cars tended to bounce and heave as they crossed the bricks, and on many occasions the frame or suspension would actually bottom out. This was expensive eventually, and to be avoided.

But cars being what they are, someone would just Have to gun the engine, "rap" the exhaust and do a little speed test. The result was a great *Whang* as the car hit the bricks.

Many people now might believe that the phrase "dragging Broadway" might have had something to do with a "drag race" from stoplight to stoplight at the time. I always believed that the term should have been taken far more literally – when we Dragged Broadway, the cars really were *dragging* on the bricks! Alas – popular culture has lost those little details, but rest assured that's the way it really was.

Rock and Roll

Fargo generated a lot of Rock and Roll bands at the time. Most were acceptable, some were actually pretty good, and every now and again one or two would hit the Big Time. Think Bobby Vee, for example.

Down at the Crystal Ballroom – also known as the Fargo Armory, but it was probably used for dancing more than military functions (the Armories built across America 1930-60 were the biggest and best public venues in many small towns) – there was a dance pretty much every weekend. The building is gone now, but it was at the foot of Broadway, south of Main, just where the hill goes down into Island Park. Sometimes there would be live bands, sometimes a DJ with records. But it was a requirement that the Young People attended the dance whenever possible.

The object was to Meet Girls/Boys. Well, that's what everybody said, and some may even have believed. But the behaviors worked in mostly exactly the opposite way.

The girls would gather in self-protective groups – think about how musk ox will gather in circles with their horns pointed outward for self-protection. It was sort of like that. We all walked around the dance floor endlessly – mostly counter-clockwise as I remember. Why that direction? I have just No idea – it was just what had always been done, and it never seemed to change.

The guys, meanwhile, also gathered in groups, though mostly smaller. The conversations followed a pattern. "Hey look at that one! She's really stacked!"

For those not currently familiar with the lexicon, Being Stacked was...hmmm...how can I put this...the Great Attractor for young American men at the time. We all read – or looked at anyway – Playboy religiously. "For the articles" of course, as we commented on the great writing to be found in it. Sure!

"Go ask her to dance," someone would suggest.

It's one thing to admire from afar, and quite another actually to Talk to a girl in her protective gaggle, much less ask one to dance. That took more courage than many of us had at the time. She couldn't be cut from the herd. All her friends would be looking – and judging. What if she said No? What recourse would there possibly be? How could one return to one's friends after such a public rejection?

No – the Much safer course was simply not to ask at all, and continue walking around and around endlessly while lusting after unapproachable beauty. Much less risk that way.

I knew kids who seem hardly ever actually to have danced at the Crystal, though many of them went there every chance they got. Inside, the non-dancers probably outnumbered the actual dancers by three to one, anyway. Those who were dancing were often those who were already Going Steady or as near to that as didn't really matter. They already had their partners selected and exclusive.

Others just sort of yearned for unrequited attention.

There was the one really big local concert cancelled, causing pretty much everyone to be depressed for a week. It was supposed to take place at the Moorhead Armory, just across the Red River, in Moorhead, Minnesota. The concert was to have featured Rock and Roll pioneers Buddy Holly, Richie Valens and the Big Bopper. But their small plane crashed in a blizzard in early February 1959, and all three died en route to that concert. I had tickets to the event, and sadly turned them in for the refund.

Sex in the Days Before the Revolution

Sex, so the adults were always telling their kids, was Bad. One thing led to another, and before you would know it the girl was either pregnant and in the Florence Crittendon Home on Thirteenth Street South over just north of Agassiz Junior High, or both participants had some horrible disease. Not to mention the social disgrace, and whatever eternal horrors were going to happen in the afterlife.

It was to be avoided At All Costs!

Yeah – right! Sure it was. The adults were lying. We knew that. So did the adults. But the idea seemed to be that if the Consequences Of Sex were unthinkable, then no one would think of them.

I have No idea why anyone ever believed that.

Fact of the matter is, we weren't always sure of all what was involved, but we were intent on trying to find out. At the time, though, finding out was not all that terribly simple or easy, in large part because there were precious few Places to go where such attempts could be made. If one didn't have a car available it got really tricky to find a place simultaneously warm and free of mosquitoes to actually attempt any epidermal contact.

A large number of our parents' generation were conceived in the back of Model As, though few ever admitted it. And a bunch of us War Babies and later on Baby Boomers were conceived during wartime romances too. Leave us not mince words – the U.S. was a hugely horny place for several decades there.

Birth control hadn't yet come on market, and condoms were – well, nearly impossible to get and tended to be kept for so long in one's wallet – mostly in hope – that if there was a chance to use them they were largely past their due date. Chancy altogether.

As a result, such sex as there was involved more talk and less actual action. But even the talk got ritualized in some quite bizarre ways.

Have a date on a weekend, and come Monday when one met up with The Guys once again, chances were better than even the conversation would sound like this:

"So – you had a hot date on Friday night?"

"Yeah – she's a really nice girl and we had a really nice time."

"Smile if you got any."

What are the chances one could Not smile at that remark? None. It always elicited a smile, which resulted in a great deal of ribald ribbing immediately thereafter. Early on, the entire idea of "getting any" was open to considerable conjecture anyway. What was the Any to be got? We knew about the three bases, but those were also somewhat vague in operation. How much of the Any could be got in the first place? Did momentary touching count, or was a full-up fondle of more than, say, 5-10 seconds required?

It was all so Very unclear.

A variation on the foregoing conversation went only mildly differently, and came without the Smile If phrase.

"So – did you get any?"

A simple No would be tantamount to admitting defeat. But an affirmation would be a lie most likely, and further besmirch the reputation of the young woman under discussion. How to answer. The face-saving and reputation-keeping answer was automatic:

"No – but I could have if I wanted to."

Now stop and think about that – being in the situation where you Could Have but...Didn't Want To??? In retrospect, it doesn't seem likely. There wasn't a One of us who, if presented with a situation where we Could Have wouldn't have Wanted To.

But it was recognized by all involved that this would keep all of the appropriate social norms in place, one's own studliness would be preserved and no one's reputation would be ruined by being seen as Easy. The social niceties being preserved, we all agreed it was time to go to class.

These influences became intertwined in some rather fascinating ways. The music was, even now in retrospect on hearing it, somewhat more than just suggestive. It wasn't the "animal beat" that some of the preachers of the time suggested would drive teenagers into all sorts of Sinning – it was the lyrics.

Wouldn't it be nice if we were older, and we didn't have to wait so long...

For what?? We all knew. And waiting so long just seemed, well....So Long!

The lyrics to the whole song were mild, as such things go now, but then – Hoo Boy! Consider:

86

You know it's gonna make it that much better when we can say goodnight and stay together...

There it was! None of this dancing around. It would be nice to do that!

But the social conventions had to be preserved:

We could be married, and then we'd be happy...

Well, yes – we Could be married, though the assurances of being happy were some ways off, and not really approachable to someone in their mid-to-late teens.

But no question – it Would be nice to deal with all that other stuff. Was there anyone at the time who didn't hear those lyrics of those (and a lot of other even more suggestive songs) and dream of Not having to Wait So Long? Not many, I'll tell you.

The music was on the car radios endlessly. We'd hop in the cars to go down to Broadway supposedly to Look For Some Girls. That was as far as the planning ever seems to have gotten, however. Three guys in a car, three girls in another car pulling up to a stoplight side by side. What's going to happen?

Nothing!

In one or the other car, someone would say "Don't look at them!" And we wouldn't. We studiously stared straight ahead, Not making direct eye contact and Maybe trying a sideways short glance with a a deliberately uninvolved expression of disinterest.

Now how is anyone supposed to make a connection with that? And how are the kids supposed to pair off anyway, being inside a steel cocoon and with a protective bunch around you? Nearly as I ever knew, little of actual consequence occurred via such bizarre behaviors.

87

So what Were we doing? Were we Looking For Love/Sex? Probably – and had it fallen into our laps we might well have taken advantage of the search.

(It came as a Huge surprise for young men to learn that girls get horny too. We were Not prepared for that. I recall one instance where a "stacked" girl was talking with one of the jocks in the hall. I was off to one side and watched as she put one hand behind her back, then very deliberately gently tugged on the sweater, tightening it against her generous breasts. The hapless guy's eyes bugged out, he sort of stammered and was, momentarily, rendered speechless. I've laughed about that educational moment ever since.)

But somehow, at least in those venues – cars, dances and Rock and Roll, nothing seemed to happen. The actual connections usually happened elsewhere – in school, and, just as often, in church groups. There were a Lot of church groups in Fargo. At one point the Youth Room in the basement of the First Methodist Church had to be closed down because it was rapidly becoming a prime make-out location, known as "the Passion Pit."

So we'd go to dances and herd with members of our own sex, avoiding direct contact with the opposite. We'd drag Broadway to meet the opposite sex but stare straight ahead. Then we'd go to church where adults admonished us that sex was Bad and make out.

Ah, those were the days.

(Special thanks to Brian Wilson and the Beach Boys for the great lyrics.)

17.

The End of High School

Starting sometime in my junior year I could see how the whole high school scene was going to end.

Mom was a creature of her own upbringing. Never having gotten past eighth grade herself, she never had the experience of going to high school during the Depression in Canada. She was off working at 14. She had no idea how times had changed, and so clung to ways she knew. In her family, discipline was strict and immediate, obedience and compliance was demanded, and the traditional way of dealing with young males was simply to throw them out to be on their own as soon as they were of working age. That was a more common pattern than many were aware after the war, but it was always her fallback position on pretty much any disagreement she had with me.

I heard the words, "If you don't like it, you can just get out!" more than once. But for a long time, getting out was simply not an option. So I bit my tongue, gritted my teeth and just waited.

Mom had never experienced anything resembling a "social life" as a young woman. Never having known what all that was about, she remained deeply suspicious of pretty much everything. Being her eldest child, I got to deal with the first blast of all of that.

During my junior year, everyone in my class was excited to attend the Prom. I figured it was to be a big deal – I had a steady girlfriend, she was a beauty, and yes – she wanted to Go To the Prom with me. I intended to attend.

Then came Mom. She didn't actually Know much more than she'd heard about Proms (and truth be told, in her narrow circle of friends, none really knew much about it) but from the movies of the time, and various magazines she'd read, Prom Night was fraught with dangers. Driving, drinking – and maybe even (shudder!) Sex! She was having none of it. She simply forbade me to go, saying "If you go, you can just get out!"

My protestations got nowhere. I wasn't going to attend the Prom, and that was the end of it. It hurt to tell my girlfriend I couldn't take her. I understood fully that she really wanted to go – I didn't blame her at all for that. So she ended up going with someone else. That burned! I did get to see her before her date picked her up – I wanted to see her in an actual Prom Dress. She was stunning!

But she went with someone else.

I put that aside to deal with later.

During my senior year, like most in my graduating class, I was involved in the whole college acceptance thing. Having been a National Merit Scholarship Finalist – one of seven in the class that year – I had some serious hope that Maybe there might be a scholarship to somewhere that would allow me to attend someplace – anyplace other than NDSU. My parents – by now my mother had remarried – made it clear that there would be No – as in None At All – financial assistance coming from them. They weren't all that well off, and it had simply never been done previously in family history on either side.

I was pretty much on my own on that one.

90

But I applied to and was accepted at several pretty good universities. It was clear I could get in. I just couldn't afford to actually go. That fact was a bitter disappointment, but I hid it from my classmates. At the time NDSU was not the Tier I institution it has become, and for one of the National Merit Scholarship Finalists simply to say that I would be attending NDSU was somehow not up to the expectation set at the time.

My senior year was a cruise, for the most part. I'd taken all of the "accelerated" classes, though at the time they did not involve getting any extra college credit for having done so. I'd taken all the "hard" subjects, to the point where there was little left in the classes available to bother with. I ended up taking "soft" subjects like Sociology – which was a less than difficult class.

There was one major big deal in my senior year that was notable – Concerto Night. The "music kids" who played in the band or the orchestra were eligible to do a virtuoso performance if they were good enough. I was in neither the orchestra nor band during my junior year, when it was necessary to declare your intention to be considered for a Concerto Night performance during the following year. Only seniors were allowed to perform.

I played piano. Played it quite well, in fact. I was good enough – and knew it.

I had taken violin lessons some years earlier from Jim Strnad. I showed precious little real talent for the violin. The fact of the matter was I really didn't enjoy playing it all that much. After one disastrous recital, I was allowed to quit.

When I approached Harlow Bergquist, the orchestra teacher, he informed me that he didn't need violins – he needed violas. I had never played the viola, but took it up over the summer by myself, learned to read the Tenor Clef adequately enough that I could challenge my way into a seat in the viola section, which made me eligible for inclusion into the Concerto Night performances.

If I was acceptable, that is. There was no assurance that I would be.

My piano teacher for years was Maria Prausnitz. Neat old German woman of the Old School of piano teaching. Practice – Practice – Practice. She made it clear that if I wanted to do a performance, I'd best be so damned good that no one could come up with a good reason to keep me out of it. We chose the first movement of the Beethoven Piano Concerto #1 in C Major. It was early enough in Beethoven's writings that it still held some of the "classical" characteristics without getting into the more emotive stuff of his later more romantic works.

But it was difficult, I tell you!

To make things more interesting and challenging, I decided that I would perform it from memory. Just me and the piano on the stage, backed by the orchestra. No one sitting beside me, no music in front of me. It was to be all or nothing – precisely the sort of challenge I have always preferred.

I practiced. And practiced. Several hours some days. Got to the point where some of it could be handled by "muscle memory" – my fingers knew where the notes were supposed to be, even if I didn't have to expend a lot of conscious energy thinking about it. That allowed me to deal with the interpretation and execution questions, going beyond a simple rote performance.

After school, I would practice on the concert grand on the stage in the auditorium. I did that every chance I had for weeks.

But...the rehearsals were not so good. I don't do particularly well at rehearsals. They lack the need to focus that an actual performance demands. There were several times when Bergquist wanted to cancel my performance, and where Mrs. Prausnitz had to personally intervene. As the time for the performance drew nearer – and I was scheduled to perform on my 18ᵗʰ birthday, it all came more together.

Then disaster!

I had been over in early May visiting my friend Sam Brekke, and we were working on his Triumph TR-3 sports car in his garage. A chisel slipped and cut the muscle at the base of my right thumb clear to the bone. It required 9 stitches to put it back together, and a rather large bandage to keep everything in place. Thumbs are important in piano playing. Critically so. It all appeared to be coming apart. Another damned disappointment was looming, and I was determined not to have to deal with it.

But it took me entirely out of the rehearsal schedule once again, and Bergquist kept saying he thought I should voluntarily withdraw. I was having none of That! I refused.

We did the final dress rehearsal a week before the actual concert. I had been exercising the thumb, stretching the stitches and keeping it as limber as possible. I could do parts of the piece before it got too tired and sore to continue. But I'd not done the entire thing.

The bandage was still on the thumb at the rehearsal. I played the piece through in its entirety. When I was done, there was blood seeping into the bandage, but I hid it from Bergquist and everyone else. In my own head and heart, I figured I was ready.

The performance went very well. I doubt I had played the piece so well ever before, and when I finished with the cadenza I had a most marvelous sense of exaltation I've not experienced before or since. I recall grinning at the keyboard as the orchestra finished up.

I'd done it!

Someone did tape recordings of those performances. I had one for years, but lost it in one of the moves. I'd love to hear it once again, but memory will just have to do. Even now, a full fifty years later, I can still play the opening bars of the concerto from memory.

As a personal triumph, it was short-lived. Mom demanded that I not go with my fellow performers to the after-concert do and should go with the family instead. I was 18 that very day, and I'd had enough. More than enough, in fact.

I went with my friends. She remained furious for weeks.

Graduation was coming up quickly, and one of the things the school parents and community had put together was the All Night Party. I intended to go. Mom forbade me to go, once again. So I heard the same thing – "If you go, you can just get out!"

That time, I got out. Packed up a few belongings, and took a room at the local YMCA, which was then located on Roberts street next to the old Grand Theater.

I'd had enough. I was always a pretty good kid, did well in school, didn't get into trouble, wasn't given to major misbehavior (other than some quite clever pranks now and again) and just had not given Mom any reason for her behavior. Years later, she told me she had been afraid of what Might happen – that these "social things" were simply beyond her ken, and rather than take a chance, she was simply going to forbid it altogether.

Nope. Not this time. She'd run my life too much, and it was time for that phase to end.

"I'm not coming to your graduation either!" were her final words as I went out the door. I don't recall if I answered. There was no real point to it.

My sister told me years later that she and my stepfather actually did wander down to the Civic Auditorium and were in the audience. I never saw them. They said nothing to me, offered no congratulations and never really mentioned it thereafter. I thought I would be angrier than I was, but that was not the case. I was fully aware that Mom was merely acting as she had been taught and had experienced during her own girlhood. It's just that her childhood wasn't mine. I simply wasn't about to allow her to dictate the rest of my life.

I did attend the All Night Party. It was good. I'm glad I went.

The next morning, it was time to start the rest of my life. I had No idea of what to do next, but was sure I'd figure something out.

As eventually I did.

PART III

18.

The Garret and the Isetta

I needed some panache.

Shortly after I left home, I became a live-in baby-sitter for the John and Marlys Hilleboe family in a house on Fourth Avenue and Twelfth Street South. Something out of a story book – my bedroom was a low-ceilinged octagonal turret on the third floor of their old Victorian house. I liked to call it a garret. I mostly watched the kids, did some housework, some cooking and even some ironing. (Didn't care for that – Marlys wanted underwear to be ironed. That just Never made any sense to me at all.)

Mom had never let me get a driver's license. Period. End of discussion. She never drove a mile herself in all her life, and never even had a ride in a car until she was 14. So cars were something Out There somewhere, and anything she didn't understand was, by inspection, Bad.

So it was only after graduation and my own emancipation that I got a driver's license, and considered buying a car. I didn't have much money, so whatever I got had to be inexpensive. But I wanted it to have character. It was the Fall of 1962, and I was just starting college at NDSU.

I found a 1958 BMW Isetta 300 for $250. It was what's now called a Microcar – it had two wheels in front about four feet apart, two wheels in back just two feet apart, was barely more than seven feet long and had one door that opened forward – that's right, to get in you stood directly in front of the car and opened the only door, which also served as the entire front of the car, hood and windshield, when shut! It had a 1-cylinder air-cooled engine displacing about 20 cubic inches and putting out about 13 horsepower, a 4-speed transmission in the left wall (the case served as an armrest) and a chain drive.

It came up for sale and it was just So Weird that I couldn't resist buying it. Plus I didn't have much money, and the price was right. It also had no heater, but I figured it couldn't be colder than walking.

Until then, I'd probably only seen an Isetta in a magazine. This was the time of reconstruction in postwar Germany, where the Isetta was made by BMW (Bavarian Motor Works). It was the era of Microcars there. (When people asked me what sort of engine it had, I said it was a V-1.) A friend at the time had a Goggomobil, another Microcar made in Bavaria, but more conventional looking. One night he and I got both our cars onto The Quad at NDSU, and were doing laps around it at about 1 a.m. Lots of sidewalks criss-crossing it, and the campus cops couldn't really drive their large cars onto it, nor could they catch us when on foot. That was a good prank, but only once. Still, not bad. I don't know anyone else who ever did that.

Anyway, the Isetta was surely the only one in Fargo at the time. And best of all, it had panache. I needed some panache.

It also had a folding sunroof, and on a couple of warm Fall days, I put my books on the seat for elevation and drove it through the campus with my head sticking out the top of the roof.

It could do 43 mph. On a good day. With a tail wind. I drove it Once the 45 miles down Highway 10 to Detroit Lakes in Minnesota. I would never care to do that again, even if it did get 63 miles to the gallon (I tested it once). With the rear wheels just two feet apart, stability was not its strong suit, and as has now been confirmed by Science, the upper Midwest is the windiest region in the nation.

That sunroof, though, did serve another good purpose.

The Isetta is small. Really small. Two people inside it had best be good friends, because you sat cheek by jowl in it. Let's just say that, to look at, this was Not the car to get laid in. Simply not enough room.

But... that sunroof. It could be folded back, and rather than get Laid, one could get Sat. Perhaps it's no coincidence that the Isetta was originally designed by an Italian, not a German. That sunroof was there for a Reason.

I'm really not trying to be offensive or shocking here. But if we are going to discuss Fargo and kids in Fargo at the time, folks ought to be aware of what was really going on, rather than pretending it wasn't. And in an Isetta, it was funny!

Alas, the Isetta was not long for this world. A few weeks after buying it, I had driven it over to my girlfriend's apartment on Tenth Street, and was signaling for a left turn into the parking lot. In the rear view mirror I saw a Chevy turn right onto Tenth Street from Thirteenth Avenue behind me, and as it did, its driver's-side rear door flew open. I became transfixed on the image in my rear view mirror as this large Chevy approached from behind with a door swinging wildly out to its left, then watched in growing horror and disbelief as the driver turned around completely (!) in his seat to close the door and drove right into the back of my car! Knocked me clear up onto the boulevard.

It was undriveable. I was heartbroken. My first car – one with real panache – and it didn't last three flaming weeks!

Two days later, I was sitting in the library at NDSU and had a slight headache. I put my head back on the chair, and couldn't lift it again. Got the attention of a co-ed across the room by waving my hand, and asked her to call the Health Center. They came by and got me to the Fargo Clinic.

Broken neck. Compression fracture of the Fifth cervical vertebra. I would recover, but it would require 3-4 months in a 4-poster neck brace. I collected about $5K for the injury, but it ended my car dreams for the rest of the year – driving before the injury was fully healed was out of the question.

(George Brekke bought the Isetta for salvage, pounded out the dents and got it running again. His son Sam, of Fargo High prankster fame, drove it for a while, but I later lost track of it. In pristine condition, those tiny little cars are now worth something like $30,000 to collectors.)

Meanwhile, I was taking several double-credit courses at NDSU – enough that I was practically a sophomore by the end of my first quarter.

Still living in the garret, I then unwisely took a part-time job at the Fargo Forum newspaper downtown. I would (try to) get up at about 5 a.m., get to the newsroom and tear down the Associated Press material that had come in overnight, tear down the perforated tapes that were an early attempt at something other than manual typesetting, take down and distribute the AP wire photos that had come in and just generally distribute any overnight material to the appropriate desks for the following day.

Occasionally on evenings, during the sports tournament season, I would sit at a typewriter and take calls with line scores from around North Dakota and western Minnesota.

On weekends, my duties were somewhat more interesting. I was an actual Copy Boy – perhaps one of that last of that genre. Reporters would type up materials, holler "Copy" and I would take it into the press room, where the linotype operators still got the material hot cast into type. Pretty much a "go-fer" job.

This was all on the heels of the accident in the Isetta. I was in a four-post head brace for most of every day, taking a fair number of pain pills to deal with the headaches, sleeping in and coming in late to work way too often. Finally Gerry Rafftery told me I was fired.

It was just my second quarter of college – we we on the Quarter system then, not Semesters – and my grades had gone to hell.

Nothing works all the time – including me.

19.

Ivers Funeral Home

If there was no one lying in state, we'd tune the radio to a Rock and Roll station and pipe it through the place on the Public Address system.

In the spring I went to work for Ivers Funeral Home and moved into the basement of a house next to what was then maybe a dry cleaner just to the south of Ivers. The room was part of my pay, and my new roommate (I'd just left the garret) was August "Augie" Zamolsky, a very well-known softball pitcher in the area.

Our job involved one evening On and one Off with alternating weekends, when were were On Call after normal operating hours. We picked up bodies and delivered them to the funeral home for embalming, and preparation for the funerals.

First time I had to do that was for a gentleman in his 80s at least. He had a hernia larger than a softball poking out from his abdomen, and was apparently in some considerable pain from it. One afternoon he placed a galvanized pail on the basement floor, climbed up on it and looped an electrical cord around a basement floor joist and his neck, then – quite literally – kicked the bucket and hung himself.

When we got there, he was down, but the cord was still wrapped tightly around his neck. We loosened it and took it off, and started to pick him up. Hanging suicides will generally inhale just prior to the act, so there was a fair amount of air still left in his lungs. When we picked him up, there was a loud moan from the escaping air.

That was startling, I tell you! I had No idea that happened. Augie just laughed and explained it. We never had another quite like it.

Another duty involved being around in the evenings for the Visitations, when Bud and Herb, the usual staff, weren't there. We wore very somber dark suits, and sat in the nice office just to the right of the entrance and wait to hear the buzzer when anyone came through the door.

If only one person was there, we simply led the visitors to the visitation rooms then stood by in case anyone needed anything or any assistance. One never knows with such things – when people break up emotionally at seeing a deceased loved one, they can simply collapse and need help.

If there was More than one of the dearly departed, we would assume a look of the deepest sorrow we could, and say in the Most solemn voice we could manage, "And whom did you come to visit this evening?" Then we would escort them to the appropriate room.

If there was no one lying in state, we'd tune the radio to a Rock and Roll station and pipe it through the place on the Public Address system. Which made for some interesting reactions when someone came in unexpectedly.

One night I caught Augie taking a nap in a coffin in the basement display room. I didn't wake him. He'd been playing softball and had pitched two no-hitters in a row and was pretty well worn out.

When there were weekend funerals, the one on duty would drive the hearse. The coffin took up pretty much all of the room, the interior was plain flat vinyl, and worst of all there was no radio. So last rides were, for the most part, silent. No Rock and Roll en route.

As jobs go, it wasn't either bad or good. It was just a job.

But not an undertaking I was interested in as a career.

20.

The 1956 Rambler Four-Door

Red and white, on the ugly side, but with a little work I modified the folding front seats so both could be folded back with one lever.

There were some places to Park out south of Fargo, down by the cemetery near the Fargo Country Club. A sort of wetland where one could pull in and it was dark, and one could get involved in some Making Out. Maybe even a little Petting.

Problem was, the Fargo Police were warned about this nefarious practice by some of the nearby residents and even the chief minister of the First Lutheran Church on Broadway. So they patrolled it several times an evening.

My funniest personal memory of being parked was one August night, not doing much that was Too serious, when up came a patrol car staffed by one of the Good Cops – a Police Auxiliary. They were the part-timers, and pretty much their only function was to cruise around looking for teenagers seeking a little make-out time, and run them off the place.

The patrol car pulled up behind us, and the cop got out and knocked on the window. We didn't have anything to button up at the time, so rolled down the window and responded as politely as possible, "Yes officer?"

He explained that some of the neighbors had been complaining about the Lovers' Lane activities, and so would we move somewhere else? Not sure how I summoned the courage to ask, but I did.

"Do you have any recommendations?" I never figured to get an answer other than "Just go somewhere else."

"Well, if you drive south on Highway 81 for about three miles, then turn right and go about a mile, then left there's a place that's pretty private."

I was astounded! A most helpful and understanding Peace Officer indeed. Wish I could remember his name – it was Hispanic sounding, if memory serves. I smile about that every now and again.

It was pretty private at that. Revisited it several times thereafter, till it got too cold.

Bless his heart! He understood, and hadn't forgotten.

Pranks to the Rambler

I had friends in college who would offer to loan me their cars on weekends, in exchange for use of the Rambler. I got to drive some really nice sports cars – Austin-Healeys, Corvettes, MGs and other sports cars, along with some fairly serious domestic cars with large engines but, alas, fixed front seats. My Rambler had No actual performance to it, and was about as plain as could be. But those seats....

Use your imagination.

Came a time when one young man whom I knew managed to score a date with a young woman from Concordia College. She was a real beauty, and he was Most proud of being able to go out with her. It was to a basketball game, if memory serves.

108

He'd set it up a week or ten days early, and he was quite pleased with himself that he'd been able to get a date with so desirable a young woman.

His request to borrow my car wasn't based on anything nefarious. He didn't have a car, mine was available, and I saw no real problem loaning it to him. And besides, he had been involved with pranking me earlier, so was due a good one. This was to be the one.

I was somewhat taken with his Personal Pride at the date, and knowing it was a Proper Lutheran Girl from Concordia College, there was an opportunity here for a Serious prank.

So – he took her to the game and parked the car. I had an extra set of keys, so could get into it while parked. While they were at the game, several buddies (names never to be disclosed) got into the car, laid the seats back and made up the interior as a bed. Sheets, blankets, pillows all properly and artfully arranged, pink cellophane inserted into the overhead light, and as a fine finishing touch, a bud vase with a rose in it on the back window parcel shelf. And the corner properly turned down.

We were parked a few cars away, in the dark. We waited.

When they came out, and opened the car door, there was a moment of shock. The girl hollered something – none of us could quite make out exactly what – and ran off into the night.

All in all, a most proper comeuppance. Can't remember if he ever forgave me.

I, too, later got a comeuppance, of sorts. A girl I was dating thought it would be Hugely funny to put her footprints on the headliner, directly above the passenger seat. We were at Detroit Lakes at the time, and I didn't see her do it.

A few days later, though, my mother noticed them. I was giving her a ride somewhere, and she was sitting in the passenger seat from which vantage point, apparently, the footprints were Hard to miss. She gave me That Look, and things were pretty chilly for the rest of the ride, which took up much the rest of the day.

The Rambler's greatest adventure, however, was yet to come.

21.

A Santa for Sears

"Santa has to visit the rest room," I told the kids still in line.

After Ivers, I sold paint, automotive supplies and hardware at the downtown Sears store. Not bad work, not good either. I was one of the army of part-timers Sears hired so they needn't pay any benefits. But over time, my sales skills were good enough that I was offered a full-time position.

I didn't want to work full-time for Sears.

But... there was one Sears job that was quite out of the ordinary.

Playing Santa Claus at Christmas.

There was a nice Santa throne just to the left of the stairway to the basement near where the toys were at that season, and I was "volunteered" to be Santa Claus.

The whole shebang – itchy nylon white beard, hot red/white suit and hat and a pillow for the appropriate round belly. In some ways it was like that Santa in the Christmas movie "Christmas Story" where Ralphy visits a Santa who comes off as a demented elf. Not quite that severe, but some days...

The best tale to come out of that, though, was an occasion when a young mommy came down and asked to talk to me. She said that in a few minutes, she was going to bring her boy Tommy down to see me, and that I should greet him by his name. I said I would do that.

Tommy showed up.

"Ho Ho Ho – why Hellooo, Tommy! Thank you for coming to visit me today."

Tommy stopped dead in his tracks. Looked at me for several seconds, then asked, "How do you know my name?"

"Why Tommy – Santa Claus knows Every little boy's name!" I responded.

He took several more seconds to process this, then said, "OK – what's my brother's name?"

Santa had no defense. Nothing to say or do, so I gave him a sucker and his mom led him off, mouthing "I'm sorry, "shrugging her shoulders as she went. Several other parents in the line cracked up. So did I. Took several minutes to get it back together. "Santa has to visit the rest room," I told the kids still in line.

I still chuckle about that one, fifty years later. I wish the very best for Tommy, and trust that he became all he could be. A kid that intuitive, skeptical and aware deserves the best the world has to offer.

I soon left Fargo on a Trip To Find America. Worked other jobs elsewhere, but none of those ever generated stories that good.

Years later in graduate school, I took several courses that discussed Employee Motivation, that suggested Work was Meaningful in some deep-seated nearly spiritual way, and that many people found great personal satisfaction from their jobs. I never got to that point. Work was mostly a way of surviving and, if you were Very lucky, would finance your spare time. I missed something, apparently.

22.

The Tour to Find America

Sam Brekke and I held Jack Kerouac in a sort of god-like status. We read On the Road *several times. Do you suppose Kerouac would have invented that way of writing if he hadn't spent his formative years growing up with that name, which had such a cool be-bop rhyme to it?*

Sometime in early 1964, I developed a case of wanderlust. It may have been driven to some extent by my deep personal disappointment when my long-time First Great Love of My Life had gone starstruck and left for New York, where she eventually married an itinerant "theater director" who had done a play at the Fargo-Moorhead Community Theater. Or some combination of that and boredom with college. Or whatever.

As many other young men at the time did, I got caught up in the idea of hitting the road to Find America. I got into my 1956 Rambler and just drove off. Didn't bother to withdraw from school. I was that alienated from the whole scene.

Toured mostly the western states. Went to California and hung out on the beaches for several weeks, did the Surfing Scene and demonstrated no real talent for it. Worked odd jobs here and there to stay alive. It wasn't hard. Migrated northward to

Oregon, where for a time I was a choker setter (a very dangerous job, and damned hard work!) for a "gyppo" logger (aka Timber Thief) out of Cottage Grove, and later worked in the Georgia-Pacific plywood mill in Springfield, while living in what I now call the People's Republic of Eugene.

While involved in these peripatetic wanderings, I got a letter from the Selective Service System, aka the Draft Board, instructing me that I was to report for a pre-induction physical.

I had what were later called "other priorities." I didn't call it that at the time, but simply stated I did Not wish to be drafted, I had No intention of being drafted, and if I could reasonably claim I never saw the letter, I was in the clear.

Sort of.

So I believed at the time. So I made a point of moving every few months and leaving no forwarding address when I did. It wasn't difficult. After the first letter, I saw only one more and threw it away unopened the very day I moved. I never saw another one.

Working in the woods and in the plywood factory cured me of any interest in Honest Manual Labor. It was boring, it hurt, my co-workers were not interesting people to spend any time with, and just generally I didn't much care for it. I know – that whole Manual Labor thing is an ongoing theme in U.S. culture, but it simply wasn't for me. So I quit.

And in the fullness of time, I ran out of money.

About the same time, the Rambler finally just died – rod bearing I think. Not worth repairing. I sold it and a few other possessions, bought a Greyhound bus ticket back to Fargo and came home.

23.

Alice's Restaurant

As a memory jogger, the reader is urged to find a copy of Arlo Guthrie's classic 1967 release, "Alice's Restaurant" – or just do an Internet search, it's right there on You Tube – and listen to it a couple of times. The album cover suggests it was about an actual incident that happened in November, 1965. The incident described herein happened in March or April of that same year.

On getting back to Fargo, I looked up several friends who had an interesting thing to tell me.

The FBI was looking for me. Apparently they thought I was a Draft Dodger.

(Mind you – that whole draft dodger thing hadn't really gotten started all that well in early 1965, the Viet Nam War was just getting into its escalation, and the anti-war/draft protest movement was nascent. I was aware of it only vaguely while in the People's Republic of Eugene. I didn't have much in the way of feeling or thought about it at the time. The Gulf of Tonkin incident was still being taken seriously. People believed that the North Vietnamese gunboats actually had attacked a U.S. destroyer, and like everyone else I figured that they had Something coming in retaliation. Certainly the U.S. could give a proper comeuppance to that small country in a fairly short time, right? It was just no big deal. I was making no great political or personal statement whatsoever.

But as for being drafted? No – I didn't much care to do that. As I said, I had Other Priorities at the time. I wanted to return to NDSU to go to school, among other things.

But….having the FBI looking for you is one thing. Having them find and arrest you is quite another. I figured, quite reasonably, that if I went to the SSS office (Selective Service System, then located on the second floor of the old Post Office) and discussed it with them, somehow we could work things out.

So on probably the second or third day of my return, I went to the SSS office, where I was greeted by a really pleasant woman, who asked "Can I help you?"

"No I don't think so," I responded. "But perhaps I can help you."

"What's your name?"

When I gave her my name, a head popped up from behind a wall of those old green/gray file cabinets that crossed the office. The guy asked, "What did you say your name was?"

I repeated my name, trying not to sound too much of a smart-ass.

But then he got into his own version of stupidity, and truly the match was on.

"We've been looking for you. Where have you been? We were thinking of getting the FBI after you."

I didn't burst out laughing, though I did think about it momentarily. I knew full well they did have the FBI after me. Their problem was, I hadn't been found. And voluntarily showing up pretty much put an end to that problem.

"I've been traveling around for the past year or so, just here and there," I responded.

"Didn't you get any of the notices we sent?"

116

A straight-up lie was in order, and it was an important one. The honest answer could have caused me a Great deal of trouble, and there was no way I wanted that. I was no fool.

"No. Never saw anything. Just figured that once I got back, I'd check back in with you folks to see what was going on. So here I am."

Perfectly plausible, as the best lies should be. Best of all, they couldn't prove otherwise. Several notices had been returned, the FBI did not or could not find me where they were looking, I had voluntarily checked in. I was, at least for the moment, off the hook.

The discussion shifted abruptly at that point.

"You need to report for a pre-induction physical," the guy said.

"When?"

"Right now. Today. This afternoon."

Ah – they were Serious about all of this. But even for this little bureaucracy, that rigorous a schedule was a bit too much.

"How about tomorrow morning?"

"I'll give you the notice, and you Be There at 8 am!" It was an order, not a suggestion.

I knew full well I was Not going to be drafted. I had a Medical Condition – pilonidal cysts. My medical history in the archives of the Fargo Clinic and St. Lukes Hospital proved it. They would become infected from time to time, drain with considerable pain, required surgery to correct, and the U.S. Army didn't want recruits with that condition in their ranks.

So, no way was I going to be drafted. I knew that. The Selective Services Board guy didn't. But he didn't make that call.

So, promptly at 8 a.m. (hadn't yet gotten into that Oh-Hundred Hours thing) I reported to the AFEES (Armed Forces Entrance Examination Station) Center near the river over by the motel, now a Howard Johnson's, east of the Civic Center in

117

Fargo. I handed in my notice, and the process started. I tried to offer my doctor's statement, but was told That Comes Later. OK – I'd wait till later.

They first gave me the Armed Forces Qualification Test. Ostensibly an intelligence test, it was supposed to take maybe an hour. I finished early.

In the next phase, they handed me a sheet where I was to list Every run-in I'd had with The Law. There was one – I spent an evening in county jail during the Seaside Riots in Oregon in 1964, when I was in a crowd of pretty much drunk college kids who were acting like drunk college kids so often did. But I gave them a false name – I didn't have ID on me – and so nothing ever showed up in a record.

But....I could see the potential here for some serious fun. After less than a minute, I took a fateful decision. I began making up a criminal record.

Nothing all that serious, mind you – things I knew were misdemeanors of no particular importance. But it was clear from the guy giving the instructions that the U.S. Army didn't care to have miscreants in its ranks. (There were stories of courts ordering people who actually Had done these crimes into the military, but I was never able to confirm even one, then or later.)

I think what probably got his attention was when I asked for a second sheet.

I didn't fill that out completely – just added maybe another half dozen lines of fake criminality, and handed it in.

(In the Alice's Restaurant song, Arlo was consigned to Group W. I was merely told to go sit in an empty room and wait till I was called. So I did that.)

Somewhat later, I was ordered to another room where, I was told, The Psychologist was going to interview me. I'd been to child psychologists ten years earlier because of some

118

hyperactivity, and I'd taken psychology classes at NDSU. But being interviewed? For a reason? Hey! This had potential.

Having not had a haircut for probably over two months, my hair was then in a reasonably severe duck tail – combed back on the sides and slicked down with Brylcreem. I was wearing a T-shirt and jeans. Think James Dean, without the sneer.

The Psychologist was a hoot! Obviously a butterbar Second Lieutenant, he wasn't much older than I. His branch insignia was Medical Service Corps. He was a New Guy! Given his facial expression when he examined both of my papers, he believed he was interviewing a Real Bad-Ass delinquent.

I gave him reason to go with that. I adopted a slouch in the chair, and an air of considerable indifference and apparent resentment.

"So, quite a history you have here."

"Yeah." A proper "yeah" delivered with a bored and slightly hostile tone.

"Why did you do these things?"

"Seemed like the thing to do at the time."

"How do you feel about them now?"

"I'd probably do them again."

The game was on. He thought he was directing the interview, but I grabbed the initiative.

"How did you get along in school?"

"I hated school!"

"Why?"

"All the teachers bossing me around, telling me what to do, how to dress and like that. I just didn't like it."

"Did you get in trouble in school?"

OK – he didn't ask When I got into trouble, and clearly I had visited Vince several times during my time at Roosevelt. But never in high school.

119

"Yeah – the teacher was always sending me to the principal's office."

"I see."

I didn't respond to that. He needed time to process this revelation.

Something you should know. I was Never a Bad Kid in school. I absolutely Loved school, was always on good terms with all of my teachers, had a Great time there, lots of friends, was involved in activities from one-act plays to the debate team to the science club to intramural sports. Just never caused any real trouble of any sort.

But he didn't know that. He pondered on for several minutes.

"What do you think about being in the Army?"

"I don't think I'd be very good at that. I get Really mad when someone starts bossing me around."

"What do you do when you get mad?"

"It depends." I let that stand, and answered no further. He pondered a bit more, made some marks on the paperwork he had, and told me I could leave.

So I went back and finished the physical, turned my head and coughed, the doctor confirmed I did have a heartbeat and my temperature was normal, and that pretty much ended the day. They never did ask me about the note from my doctor about the cysts. With a bunch of others, we were told we could leave. So I did.

It was maybe six weeks later that I got another envelope from the SSS Board office. I opened it with some foreboding. This was what a draft letter would come in. But it was, to my considerable relief, Not a draft notice.

It was a draft card, and my status was 4-F. That meant that sometime after the lame, halt, sick and blind became soldiers, I might be called up. But it also meant there was No Way I was going to be drafted, and I could go back to my Other Priorities in life.

Still, I was curious. I could see where they might list me as 4-F because of my broken neck from the car accident in 1962. But that was only a compression fracture, had healed completely and wasn't cause for a deferment on that basis. They never had seen the doctor's letter about the pilonidal cysts. So it was unclear why I was 4-F, and I wondered. So I called the SSS office and asked. The same nice woman who had greeted me earlier gave me the reason.

"Well, your intelligence test came out just fine. Quite good, in fact. And physically you are certainly in pretty good shape. But (this with a tone of some regret, perhaps remorse – I wasn't sure) I'm afraid you are considered Morally Unfit."

I nearly howled with laughter, but suppressed the urge. I thanked her and hung up the phone. Then I laughed, long and hard, till tears ran down my face.

They had bought it! They'd bought the story! I could scarcely believe it.

Please understand – when I went to the AFEES station, I had No intention at all of taking this route. The medical statement would have gotten me the exact same deferment anyway. But this potential came up, and once the opportunity was there, I couldn't resist following it.

Morally Unfit. Me?

Hilarious!

So I was off the hook. It was, at the time, no big deal to me. I wasn't going to be drafted anyway, so the reason wasn't all that important. Then.

It became important later.

Coda: During all of 1967 and most of 1968, I showed that 4-F draft card to my fellow soldiers, and later, NCOs (Non-Commissioned

121

Officers) in the NCO club in Phu Loi, Republic of Viet Nam. I was the only one who had a genuine 4-F card. It got me a lot of free drinks from my comrades, and they Loved the story behind it. They also thought I was nuts for enlisting anyway, when I could have stayed out. They were probably right.

24.

Pranks Be to Baby Jesus!

The problem here is – How Do You Give It Back?

It's a good thing there is a Statute of Limitations.

For a while, I lived in a "garden level" apartment over on 19th Street North. It was infamous, and rumor had it that it was considered Off Limits to students from NDSU, Moorhead State, Concordia, Interstate and Dakota Business Colleges and the local Moler Beauty College.

The entire building would throw a Blowout – and sometimes they got a little out of hand and noisy. But came one Christmas party...

I passed out in my room, and awoke next morning with a pretty bad hangover. Felt just Terrible! Stumbled out into the living room area, and just like that, Things Got Worse. Not just Worse – Really worse! Worse in Spades!

There, in the living room, was a smallish statue of a donkey, a man in a jeweled robe and on the couch, dressed in swaddling clothes, was... The Baby Jesus!

We turned on the television news, and the newscast was full of the story. Someone had gone to the Nativity Scene at the Foot of Broadway – in front of what was then the JC Penney's building – just south of the tall bank, the First National, now Bell State Bank, and just slightly north of the Northern Pacific railroad tracks, with the Woolworth building directly west of it, that entire area was ofttimes called the Foot of Broadway – someone had gone to the Nativity Scene there and Stolen The Baby Jesus! It was an Outrage! Someone Had To Pay!

And here He was – in my apartment! Seriously, I had No idea of how He got there. I did know He couldn't stay there long. We wrapped him up in more swaddling clothes, put Him and the donkey and the Wise Man into the trunk of a friend's car and drove it over to the other side of the NDSU campus while we tried to figure out what to do.

You see – the problem here is... How Do You Give It Back? Given the Outrage going through Fargo at the time, none of us wanted to go to jail for Stealing The Baby Jesus. Especially when we didn't do it. Honest – we didn't!

We waited, got back to the car, took the three statues out to a local shop – might have been the county shop, or the city shop or some other shop. I really don't remember. But we put them in the dark, out of sight, and from a pay phone called a local radio station to tell them where The Baby Jesus could be found.

Nothing ever came of it. We never knew for certain who did it, but if the initials JJE spark any memory in readers, that'd be a lead worth following.

Scary prank, though! Maybe the best ever pulled on me.

Hmmm, I wonder if that guy with the gorgeous date from Concordia somehow caught wind of that party...

25.

The Bison Hotel

No story about the Fargo of that time would be complete without a discussion of The Bison Hotel.

It was then located on Broadway, just to the south of the Great Northern Railway crossing. It was an old hotel, but it had a restaurant in it. The restaurant was open 24 hours a day.

The big thing folks remember about the Bison Hotel, though, was the steak special on the menu. A smallish T-bone with a potato and side salad for $1.09. That is not a misprint – it was called the Dollar Nine.

Let's be clear with this. This was a Tough cut of meat, over-enzymed to make it cuttable with a steak knife. It was thin. It only came well done – the idea of any other treatment would not have been considered.

Those of us in Fargo who stayed out beyond normal hours spent a fair amount of time in the Bison. There was a crowd of regulars who were there several times a week after 9 p.m., and certainly after midnight. Staying for a long time carried with it a smallish benefit – if you ordered your Dollar Nine before the 10:30 waitress shift change, then waited and after the new shift came on you ordered something smaller, you could cadge the Dollar Nine without paying for it. Seriously.

I knew three or four guys at the time for whom this was the only substantial meal of the day. Nobody ever said anything about it – least of all to the hotel management.

There was also a lively trade that went on with catsup, mustard, salt, pepper and sugar. The full containers would disappear and be replaced with empties, which would naturally be refilled in due course. It saved money for a fair number of people.

Legend had it that Bob Dylan, then known as Robert Zimmerman, was a regular at the Bison Hotel in 1959. That was before my time, but it did add a certain panache to our hanging about there some years later.

The regulars at the Bison Hotel as of 1963 or so were still quite notable. The local Rock and Roll groups would come there early in the mornings after they played their local gigs. I recall Marc Wroe showing up in ski pants – with stirrups on the feet. It was the most extreme of the tapered look favored by avant-garde young men at the time, and folks thought that was quite stylish. John Leppart would show up, but as a general rule he was mostly involved in a downer of some sort, and seldom said a lot save to his band friends.

My most notable Bison Hotel character had to be Tom Connoboy. His dad was a mild-mannered accountant in town, and the family lived over on Eighth Avenue North, between Ninth and Tenth Streets. I first ran across Tom some years earlier when he was a ham radio operator – and I was fascinated by the radio set-up in his upstairs room.

At the time, Tom drove a 1956 or 1957 Ford convertible – red, with a red and white interior. It was the only one in town just like that, and there was no mistaking who it was if you saw it on the street.

There was one night, possibly in late October or early November, when it started to snow for the first time that Fall. He came into the Bison about 2 a.m., and there hadn't yet been much accumulation – maybe a half inch or so. But it was coming down pretty hard.

In a loud voice, Tom addressed the entire restaurant:

"I want you to know that if it snows more than one inch tonight, I am driving to California."

The wait was on. Long about 3:30 or 4 a.m., the radio said that 1.05 inches had fallen at Hector Airport.

Tom bid us all farewell and left the restaurant, got in his car and drove off. We all thought he was kidding.

He wasn't.

Four days later, someone in the restaurant got a call from Tom. He was in Los Angeles, and said he would see everyone again, maybe in April.

I was sitting in the restaurant one night, when the pay phone – which was located at the far end of the place down near where the bathrooms were – rang. Someone down there picked it up and answered.

"There's a long distance call here for Don Homuth."

I took it. It was from a friend I'd left in Oregon during my western tour a year earlier. We'd first met up some time earlier while in Fargo, and he was aware I spent a fair amount of time in the Bison Hotel.

It wasn't so much that he called the hotel to find me. That happened maybe several times an evening to various people.

It was that I was there to get it!

Over time, especially when I went back to school and didn't have as much time to spend Hanging Out, the attraction of the place faded. Then I enlisted in the Army, went to Viet Nam, and when I got back it held no further attraction at all.

But it still holds a warm place in memory.

127

PART IV

26.

Too Clever by Half

As much fun as the episode with the SSS Board was, it turned out that I had screwed myself.

I enrolled back at NDSU that summer, fully intending to get back into the Science career I had sought three years earlier, and got back into the swing of classes and lessons.

Then I met this fellow – Major Robert A. Hansen, U.S. Air Force. He either was part of or was just coming to the AFROTC (Air Force Reserve Officer's Training Corps) Detachment at NDSU as an instructor for the ROTC students. He suggested that I might consider enrolling in AFROTC and consider becoming a U.S. Air Force officer after graduation.

As I said earlier, I had always intended to serve at some point, but just on My terms and not the military's. So in the Fall, I did just that. I took to it – enjoyed the classes, did the Drill Team for a while, and toward the Spring quarter of 1966 applied for entrance to Advanced AFROTC. I had the grades for it. I had a mentor in Major Hansen, and it looked as though it would all work out OK.

On the physical side, I got the pilonidal cysts excised. It was a Very painful recovery from that, but unless it was done there was no way I would ever be accepted. In having the operation, I would thereafter be medically eligible to be drafted, so there was a certain element of risk involved. No matter.

(This is precisely the same medical problem that kept Rush Limbaugh from being drafted. He didn't have his removed until after the war was over.)

My "fiancé" at the time – a really cute blonde Home Ec major – and I got crossways during the recovery. While I still had several stainless steel stitches in my hinder, she got all bothered that I wouldn't come down to the train to meet her coming back from Williston. It simply hurt too much to do that. She didn't believe me. Or something. We broke up over that.

Turns out the United States Air Force does a pretty thorough security/background check on its applicants, and wouldn't you just Know, up popped that old 4-F status from the Draft Board. And the reason – Morally Unfit – was still on the paperwork.

Well! The USAF can't have its ranks sullied by someone who even Might be morally unfit, can it? So my application was rejected. Major Hansen and the CO of the detachment and I had a long conference, in which I told the same story as in these chapters.

But the Air Force was adamant. No Way were they going to admit this moral miscreant into their training program. Who Knows how its personnel would be sullied just being anywhere near such a person?

Major Hansen flew down to Maxwell Air Force Base to plead my case personally. He told me later that he believed I would make a fine Air Force officer, with some of the rough edges smoothed off. He may have been right. It just wasn't to be. Maxwell ended it once and for all and said No.

I was shattered. Truly. I had come to believe that This would be my life's true calling. I'd been an airplane freak since I was ten years old. In art classes, I would draw pictures of airplanes. When I had to give a report on something in front of the class, it was always about airplanes. I all but memorized the Ground Observer Corps airplane spotters manuals (the GOC's local station in Fargo was in the old Roosevelt School building just north of the one I attended). I still remember aircraft because of that all these years later.

I didn't even want to be a fighter pilot. I wanted to fly the C-5 Galaxy cargo plane – a great Huge thing that dwarfed everything else in the inventory then, could haul large cargo amounts across great distances. The cockpit of it looked So small from the outside. But it just wasn't going to happen.

I am not normally given to depression, but that was depressing. Casting about for another military service that might offer the chance to fly, the Army ROTC program beckoned, so I transferred into it and applied for its officer program.

This was different. The Viet Nam War was then heating up in earnest, escalation was happening, the Big Green Machine was looking for officer candidates and there I was. (It's tempting to consider the comparative moral fiber of the Air Force and the Army, but I won't.) Once entered, I just didn't much care for it. Part of it was that the Army cadre at NDSU just weren't nearly as interesting as was Major Hansen. Talking with them was, frankly, downright boring. They took themselves Very seriously – which was acceptable under the circumstances. But not to a 21-year-old like me.

I cancelled the application to the final two years, and the detachment XO said it was too bad that I was leaving, but had I ever considered the Warrant Officer Training Program for helicopter pilots? No – I hadn't. Tell me more.

Within only a few weeks, I was back down at the AFEES station taking the ARWAB test – the Army Rotary Wing

Aptitude Battery. I did well on it – Really well, in fact. Highest score they'd ever seen. The U.S. Army would be Proud to take me, and would even waive the 4-F classification.

Well, OK. So much for being Morally Unfit, I guess.

So I finished out summer school in 1966, finished up some work I was doing for Dr. Andy Terranova at the USDA Radiation & Metabolism Laboratory out on the north end of the campus, and one early September morning in 1966 I got on my bike (I'd been riding a ten-speed around town ever since I'd arrived back from Oregon) and pedaled to the AFEES station. From there I was flown to Minneapolis, then to Dallas, and then – by one of what had to be the last DC-3s still in commercial service – to Ft. Polk, Louisiana for basic training.

The idea was that I'd finish there, then go to an initial helicopter training base in Texas, and if I passed that, on to Ft. Rucker, Alabama, for the advanced training and to be made a Warrant Officer flight officer.

I liked the idea of being a Warrant Officer. You'd get treated like a real officer, get almost the same pay, just fly the helicopters, but have no command responsibilities and just be less available to be jacked around. Or so I was told.

Basic was challenging. I was a tad overweight – not a lot, but enough so that the physical training was just difficult enough to leave me really tired by the end of the day. By virtue of my earlier ROTC involvement, and the fact that I'd been on the Drill Teams, I was made a Squad Leader in my platoon. Got to wear three stripes on a black armband. Didn't have to do KP (Kitchen Patrol). Heckuva deal!

I took good care of my guys. There were some who had considerable trouble with the close order drill, and I'd work with them in the late afternoons individually to help them with the movements. My squad could handle that Very well.

One incident stands out, though.

It came time to qualify on the rifle range. Our Senior Drill Sergeant was named Falby. He was the very Model of an Army drill sergeant. Tall, fit, close-trimmed graying hair, a voice like a file on metal and was forever challenging the recruits to be as good as he was. At anything.

The morning of rifle qualification, Falby was in front of the entire company, and gave his challenge –

"Is there any one of you Young People who thinks they can beat my score on the rifle range?"

Without quite thinking it through, I raised my hand.

"Home-youth (that's how he pronounced my name) – Get Up Here!" I got up there.

Peering down from the lectern, he said, "Do YOU think you can beat me on the rifle range?

"Yes Senior Drill Sergeant!" This was said in a Loud Military Manner.

"Would you like to place a bet on that?" asked Falby.

"What would you Like to bet, Senior Drill Sergeant?"

"I'll bet you a good cigar you Can't beat my score."

"I'll take that bet, Senior Drill Sergeant!"

"Get back to your squad," ordered Falby. I got back to my squad.

In the deuce-and-a-half on the way to the range, my friends said they thought I was nuts. No One ever challenges a Senior Drill Sergeant. The other lesser-ranked drill sergeants made it quite clear that they Knew I wasn't going to win the bet. Be Damned if I was going to let Any drill sergeant issue a challenge and have No one in the unit willing to take him up on it, even if he was going to lose. I didn't mind losing to a pro, but I wasn't going to let one intimidate me.

They were right. It wasn't even close.

I was the subject of a lot of harassment later on. Returning to the Company Area, we all went to chow and showered, and

135

had some time off to clean weapons and gear, etc. I did all of that early, and then went to the Orderly Room and asked to see the First Sergeant – the only NCO who outranked Falby.

"What do YOU want?" he growled. "You lost to Falby."

"Yes, first Sergeant. I request permission to go to the PX."

"Now why do You want to go to the PX?" he asked. No one got to go to the PX in Basic, and it required a pass to be away from the company area.

"I bet Senior Drill Sergeant Falby a good cigar, and I feel I should pay the bet as soon as possible."

It took a minute while he considered that, then he told the company clerk to write out a PX pass for me and he signed it. The bus to the main PX area was due to come by in half an hour, so I caught it and went. It was, by that time, about 1:00 p.m. or so – that's thirteen hundred hours, as I was then fast learning to say.

The PX area was great. First thing I did was to buy the best, most expensive cigar in the tobacco shop – one of those fancy ones that came in a metal tube with a picture on it. It might have been an Antony & Cleopatra – I vaguely remember that brand.

Then I went to the snack bar and had the first Real hamburger and French fries I'd had in weeks. And went to the ice cream store and bought a Real ice cream milk shake and took a while drinking it. Caught a movie – don't remember what it was. Wandered over to the library and read some magazines.

It was a Great afternoon. I felt for several hours like a Real Person. Caught the 6 p.m. bus back to the company, and reported back in.

The First Sergeant had gone home. Only the E5 drill sergeant was holding down the place as CQ (Charge of Quarters). He asked where I'd been and I handed him my pass and told him I was buying Falby's good cigar so I could pay off my bet. He laughed, and said he'd heard about that. "What," he inquired, 'took you so long? You've been gone about 5 hours."

"I had to do some comparison shopping to make sure I got the best cigar on the post."

It worked! They bought it! I had a Whole Afternoon to myself, and all it really cost me was the supposed chagrin of losing the bet, and the small price of a reasonably good cigar.

A basic trainee doesn't get many chances like that. I never got another one. But that one was good enough to carry me through the rest of Basic Training.

With one exception, and that was a big one.

27.

What Goes Around

...keeps on going around.

In my first sophomore year at NDSU (I took several double credit courses during my freshman year, and was pretty much a sophomore by the end of the first quarter), I played cards in the Student Union. I played a Lot of cards. Bridge, whist and sometimes pinochle. It got to the point where my card group had a table that everyone knew was more or less reserved for us – right on the left side of the door nearest the stairs in the main room of the snack bar. (The place has been remodeled since then. It's not there any more.)

Much as I hate to admit it, I'd skip classes to play cards. I was going through some of that My Girlfriend Left me depression thing. Needless to say, my grades suffered some. But I did get pretty good at bridge and whist. Hold that thought.....

After joining the Army, I was in Basic and well along, when we came up against something called the Pugil Stick drill. Supposedly this was supposed to teach some sort of bayonet and/or hand-to-hand rifle training where the rifle became a club, and you just beat the other guy with it when you got close. I always figured to shoot them instead, but this was something we Had to do.

It started as one-on-one, then three-on-two, then the worst – two on one. I was the one.

The three-striper Drill Sergeant doing the exercise chose two little guys from the Chicago South Side in my squad to take me on, and told them to put me on the ground. They were small, but fast. Very fast!

I didn't last ten seconds.

One got behind me, and the other in front. The guy behind hit the back of my head at the same instant the guy in front connected with my chin and I was Out. Like a broken light.

After being checked out by the medics, I was told I had to report to the hospital, where they looked for a concussion and didn't find anything serious. But they were Most concerned that I'd been unconscious for maybe 15-20 seconds. I remained there for observation for several days.

So much for going to helicopter pilot school.

Turns out the Army has a regulation that if there is Any period of unconsciousness at all, that would preclude the individual from trying to pilot Any aircraft for a period of six months. If there had been no other problem, you'd be re-evaluated and brought back to your previous flight status once again. So, they told me, I couldn't go to primary flight school.

But… it would be All Right, they said. I'd be sent to Ft. Rucker, Alabama, where I'd be trained as an aircraft mechanic instead. And wouldn't that be great? Frankly, no. I'd signed up to become a helicopter pilot, not a blamed mechanic and bubble polisher.

Had I known then what I know now, I could have requested and gotten an immediate discharge. Under the Warrant Officer flight program, I didn't Have to stay in if I couldn't for medical reasons. (The medical reasons were Being Unconscious – the

Basic Training knockout. The Army flight program was deeply suspicious of post-concussion problems.) But I didn't know that, so I shrugged and figured whatthell – I have to go where they tell me. So Ft. Rucker it was.

The Viet Nam War was rapidly escalating. Lots of helicopters going to Viet Nam, joined by Lots of helicopter mechanics. Yep – I got orders to go to Viet Nam at the end of December of 1966. Nothing I could do about it – just had to go.

Got to Long Binh Replacement Depot, waited several days, got put on a helicopter to another base in Phu Loi and reported to the Headquarters of the 11th Combat Aviation Battalion. They had three Huey companies, two Chinook companies and I was apparently going to become a mechanic. I didn't Want to do that, but it didn't matter.

Sitting on my duffel bag on a hot day just outside the building, I was contemplating what insidious twist of fate was befalling me, when I heard a voice saying "Which one of you is Homuth?"

The guy asking was a pleasant-looking fellow with a single stripe on his arm. I put up my hand and was told to follow him. I followed him.

Inside the white and brown building, there were several other guys at their desks, and they stopped work to say hello. Introductions were made, and I learned the pleasant looking fellow with the single stripe I'd just followed in, my first contact in country, was one Private First Class Vic Bary.

"My first question is, can you play bridge?" Vic asked. I suspect I looked stunned. "The reason why we ask is that our fourth for the bridge game is leaving, and we need someone else who can."

"Yes, I can play bridge."

"What conventions do you play?

"I can play Gerber, Scheinwald and Flugenscheiss."

Now the first two are Insider Baseball for bridge players – or were at the time. The third is a German phrase that means....oh, you can figure out for yourself what it means. It just means that every now and again, I might throw in a bid that makes just No sense at all. You know – flugenscheiss.

"Next question," Vic asked. "Can you type?"

"Yes, I can type."

"Show me." He sat me down in front of a wide-carriage Underwood 5, essentially the same as my Dad had provided to me to practice on years earlier. I typed something from memory. He handed me a pre-typed paper and told me to copy it. I copied it. He handed me a form and watched as I set up the typewriter so the letters would fit in the spaces. It wasn't hard.

"OK." Vic said. "Next question. How badly do you want to be a mechanic?"

"I don't want to be a mechanic at all," I replied. "Never did. It's just what I'm stuck with."

"Fine," said Vic. "OK – here's the deal. We work in battalion headquarters. The duty isn't bad, but it has to be done correctly. We work on personnel records, promotions, pay, leave and all that stuff that has to be handled on behalf of everyone. The personnel officer is kind of a prick, but if you do the job he probably won't bother you much. We live in hooches. They aren't very nice, but they're better than a bunker. We have hooch maids who do the laundry, shine the boots and tidy things up several days a week. You have to pay for that out of your own money. So... do you want to be a clerk?"

Without hesitation, I answered. "Who do I have to kill?"

So, two previous threads of my life came back together. The card playing was Not a total waste of time at all. And the typing my Mom had me take a decade earlier paid off too.

Thanks Mom! We had No idea that typing would keep your boy out of the mechanic duty.

141

Later on, I asked Vic why he had called on me in the first place. He said they were going through my 201 file and looked at my score on the AFQT (Armed Forces Qualifications Test — the one I'd taken just before making up a criminal record for myself two years earlier, that fateful spring morning in Fargo). When they also saw that I'd had two years of college, they'd figured if I could play bridge and type, I might just fit in OK.

Heh! All of this stuff about how well the U.S. Army runs is apparently true, then. This was sheer happenstance, blind luck and any other terms you'd like to use to describe it. I, however, was not about to gainsay the outcome. And so, for several months, I settled into the duty – a personnel clerk. I did it competently and fast.

In the meantime, I watched carefully as the helicopter units did what they did, talked with the flight crews and pilots, and learned a lot more about what it was to be a helicopter pilot or flight crew member.

Sometime about April or so, I got a TWX (Armyspeak for overseas message) from Ft. Rucker, the HQ of the Army flight training program. Seems as how my six month period had gone by, there had been no further problems, and upon being checked out by the battalion flight surgeon, I would be transported back to the U.S. to begin my flight training program once again.

Ummmmmm....this was a lot Less attractive a prospect than it had been 7-8 months earlier. By now I had a pretty good idea of what being a helicopter pilot in combat was all about. I'd seen the casualty and accident reports, including the pictures.

I figured it this way – Had I gone back to flight school, I'd have spent another four months or so in training. Upon becoming a Warrant Officer, I'd have a 6-Year commitment to fulfill from that point forward.

142

But if I stayed where I was, I had already done 8 months of a 24-month enlistment, and could be out in less than a year and a half.

This was a No-Brainer.

My entry into flight training had to be voluntary. I didn't. I told the battalion S-1 that I'd decided Not to take advantage of the Army's kind offer, and I'd stay where I was, thanks all the same.

So there's the third tieback. The typing classes a decade earlier worked out. Playing cards too much in college worked out. And getting knocked out in Basic Training worked out too. I couldn't see that at the time. Luck is good. Problem is you can't really count on it, but then you ofttimes have No idea that it's happening.

My administrative duties during 1967 were a piece of cake, relatively speaking. The base would be attacked with rockets and mortars now and then, but one would have to be very unlucky to have a problem. There's a lot to be said for cowering in a bunker when the Incoming is on the way.

I did that more than once.

Came Thanksgiving, and the Army offered us a pretty neat deal: If I extended my overseas tour, and offered to remain in Viet Nam for another six months, I could go home for Christmas with my family on a special leave, not charged against my normal leave time. By that time, I really wanted to see my family and friends in Fargo again, and that seemed too good to pass up. So I extended my tour.

During all of 1967, an elementary school class at a parochial school in Moorhead wrote personal letters to me a half dozen times. The class was taught by Randi Olsen – Alf Olsen's daughter (he was a much-respected writer and photographer for the Fargo Forum) – a classmate of mine at NDSU. I answered each letter individually with a handwritten response from Viet Nam.

I didn't tell them I was coming home. Randi and I worked it out to be a surprise. One morning, she told the class she had a surprise for them. And I walked in the door in uniform.

To this very day, I well remember the immediate silence and sharp intake of breath from the kids. Then that drawn-out word – "Do-o-n!" The visit with the kids was only wonderful. Downright heartwarming, in the very finest sense of the term.

It was some years later that I was met by a young woman in West Acres, the main shopping mall in Fargo, who asked me if I was Don Homuth. "Yes," I answered – "I am."

"I'm one of the kids in Randi Olsen's class you wrote to, and I want you to know that I've kept all those letters and still read them every now and then, just to remind me of being in contact with an American soldier in wartime."

What can one say to that? Turns out it's quite possible for a heart to be Re-Warmed all unexpected-like. But it's another example of how so many of those Fargo threads kept moving apart and coming back together for so many years. What goes around does come back around, but chances are you may well not recognize it when it does.

28.

Dear John... er, Don

Several of the people involved are still alive and living in Fargo, so to spare them the embarrassment of having to admit they were ever involved with me, I'm not mentioning names.

Sometime in August 1966, I got engaged. Lovely young woman, of a Good Fargo Family to remain unidentified. Red hair, freckles, really smart, well-spoken. I thought, and still think, the world of her. We had been involved in some joint school-related activities at NDSU, and things just sort of progressed from there.

I gave her a diamond ring – a very Small diamond, since neither I nor my family had much money. But I meant it.

A few weeks prior to leaving for Viet Nam, her family invited me over for dinner. This was a major big deal. I always got the sense that her Dad – maybe her Mom too, but she hid her feelings rather well – disapproved of me. Probably for good reasons – not the least of which was that I was not a Catholic.

(Keeping things in balance, my Mom came from an anti-Papist family with a long history of anti-Catholicism in Canada. Probably because the Catholics were French. We're all still living with the religious wars of 17th Century Europe in some ways.)

As things progressed that day, several buddies of mine decided to take me to the M&J Steak House out in West Fargo (one of their Dads owned the place at the time) and got me plastered. Not falling-down-throwing-up-in-your-shoes drunk. Just drunk to the point where I would act silly. After several hours of that, one of them drove me back to my house on 5th Avenue South and poured me out into the front lawn. I could walk, but certainly not drive.

My girlfriend's house was Waythehellandgone over to the North Side, just west of the old VA hospital. I was due there in less than an hour.

So I rode my ten-speed. The details are somewhat hazy – it was difficult to maintain balance and directional control simultaneously. But I got there OK. Her father wondered where my car was. I told him, trying to suppress a grin, that it was a nice day and I felt like riding my bike instead. I don't think he bought it.

Dinner that evening was a challenge, I tell you. (I have never done a lot of drinking, and in my entire lifetime have actually been drunk probably less than ten times, outside of being in Viet Nam.) I was at that goofy place – where everything seemed funny, and I spent the entire evening trying not to laugh. (I do recall thinking that the word Broccoli sounded hilarious. No – I don't know why. It just did.)

All through the dinner, her father kept looking at me strangely. I suspect he knew what was going on. Apparently he wasn't going to embarrass his oldest daughter in front of his family, and I've always admired him for that.

(Even just a couple of days ago, in a phone call to the same guy who got me plastered, he recalled that incident and laughed heartily about it. Especially the part about riding my bicycle several miles across Fargo while faced. No easy accomplishment.

146

Ah well....)

We stayed in touch, she and I, all through my training and well into my deployment to Viet Nam. For some months, we quite literally wrote to each other every day.

Then came that period when her letters stopped entirely. Went on for about six weeks, anyway. I knew what was coming, and so did my friends. Nothing to do but wait it out till The Letter came.

It eventually did – told me all about how she'd gone back to her high-school sweetheart, and they had decided to get married, and how her fiancé was going to work in her Dad's business (I suspect her Dad knew I would Never do such a thing) and how she was So sorry and wished me all the best, and hoped I'd be OK in the war...yadda yadda.

Well, that stung! Even though I'd been expecting it, to be confronted with the reality hurt a bit. But... what to do.

My roommate was the battalion chaplain's assistant. Nice kid! Neither of us smoked, and that was good. He intended to go to a seminary some day and become a Minister of the Gospel in his own turn. A veritable good example for everyone to follow.

I took my girlfriend's picture out of my wall locker, looked at it one last time and tore it up and threw it in the burn barrel. No sense mooning over the matter – she had left and that was the end of it. But...what to do next?

I had one of those small refrigerators in the hooch – we called personal quarters hooches – anyway, I kept a couple of cans of ginger ale in the small refrigerator. I also kept a fifth of Jack Daniels Black Label – for sipping purposes only. (My compatriots would have slugged it down completely, but I was somewhat older – by four or five years – than most of them, and considerably more civilized at the time.)

147

It was time to get plastered. The occasion was appropriate, the motivation sufficient, and all I needed was someone to drink with. (I knew full well that solitary drinking is a Very bad practice, and I've never done it in my life.)

My hoochmate came in the door, and I asked him "Do you have plans this evening?"

"No," he answered. "Why?"

"I just got a Dear John letter, and I need to get drunk, and I need a friend to drink with, and you're it."

"I don't drink," he said.

"I know – but tonight I want you to make an exception for a friend."

"I can't do that."

"Oh sure you can. Look – I know you're planning to be a minister someday. Tell me – do you know anything about Sin? Have you Ever gotten drunk, or gotten laid or deliberately done something Sinful?"

He was puzzled at that, and allowed that how no – he really hadn't that he could remember.

"Well, how do you expect to preach to anyone about Sin if you don't know the first damned thing about it?"

Now that's a simple enough argument to see through, but at least on this occasion it didn't occur to him to make it.

"I don't know. I've never really thought about it."

"Well," I responded in the Most reasonable manner I could come up with, "Tonight's your night. You will be with a friend, your friend Needs your companionship, we won't be at one of the girlie bars in town and we aren't driving anywhere. There isn't that much to drink, and it'll be OK."

It worked. He said OK. We went to chow, came back, I took the ice cube tray out of the small refrigerator and we commenced to demolishing most of the fifth of Jack Daniels.

I can't say our conversation was meaningful. Fact of the matter is, I don't recall most of it. I do recall a nice sense of friendship – that my hoochmate was willing to sacrifice a considerable life-long predisposition not to drink in order to provide solace to a friend in mildly dire straits. (I've lost track of him since. Wish I could find him. Tried, but couldn't.)

Somewhere in a forgotten U.S. Army archive (remember the final scene in *Raiders of the Lost Ark*?) there is buried a CQ Report (CQ stands for Charge of Quarters, a deliberately vague term – think of someone who had to stay awake overnight in case anything important happened, and who knew to whom to report it and could file a report on his own) from our unit. That's a report of all the goings-on in the unit and it's kept by the company clerk and signed off by the First Sergeant. I've read the one for that evening, and don't remember the exact wording involved. But it was something like this:

0230 hours. SP4 Homuth and SP4 Anderson were found on top of the bunker outside unit headquarters, singing "God Save The Queen." The CQ and runner put them to bed.

So there's an official record out there somewhere. Or was, anyway. I've heard there may have been a fire meanwhile.

It didn't Quite end at that.

He was the chaplain's assistant. I played the chapel organ for the two Sunday morning services.

We showed up a half hour before the first service, and the chaplain immediately figured out what had happened, just by looking at us. We were hung over. Not badly, but enough so that it was obvious what had been going on.

"Having a little fun last night, were we?"

Dave answered first. "Don got a Dear John and one thing led to another and…"

"I understand fully," said the chaplain. "Under the circumstances, getting plastered might have helped, but it won't

149

for long." Clearly he had something in mind, but I had no idea what.

Turning to me, he said "Do you need to talk about this at all?"

"No," I responded. "If she wants to go, she'll go. She's gone. He's there and I'm here and there's no way in hell to deal with that." (I knew even then, as I learned later in graduate school, that Propinquity is the only really important social variable anywhere. Nothing to do but get on with it.)

The chaplain let it go at that.

He did, though, make one change in the hymn to be sung that morning. The first one was changed to "Holy, Holy, Holy" – the old standard.

It was a small chapel. The speakers to the organ were very near the bench. When I got to the phrase "Lord God Almighty" I felt it through my entire body, though not as the hymn itself intended as a paean of praise to the divine. It was more of an expletive about the nature of things.

Interestingly, the hangover disappeared immediately after the services. (As near a faith-healing miracle as I've ever experienced.) I never got depressed about the Dear John letter, and in fact never really gave it much thought thereafter. Viet Nam didn't allow for a lot of distractions at the time.

Later on, after I got back, I saw her and her husband in the Student Union at NDSU. I got word that her husband was now working for her father (better him than me) and over time now pretty much runs the business. They had kids, probably are grandparents now and are quite happy. For which I say, in all true sincerity, Good On Them!

Even now, some 45 years later, I am still pleased that even for a while and at that time, a young woman like that thought enough of me to consider a lifelong relationship. It probably wouldn't have worked out. But it was a Good Thing anyway.

150

Best thing is that it left me with this quite nice story – one not all that unusual for American soldiers deployed into a war. I could have gotten along without it, but having experienced it personally, it gave me a pretty good understanding of others when it happened to them. When I became a Sergeant myself, and was responsible for the welfare of a group of guys who had it happen now and then, I was able to talk to them with the Voice Of Experience.

No regrets.

At all.

29.

December 25th, 1967

I'd been in Viet Nam for eleven months and had voluntarily extended my duty tour so I could return home to spend Christmas with my family in Fargo. I would return to war in ten days.

How clearly I remember the Christmas services that year. I'd been away seemingly forever, and the half-round chapel in the First Methodist Church seemed like something from a nearly-forgotten memory. The warm wood tones, the maroon curtain that covered the organ pipes behind, the Christmas decorations on the columns in their green and red, the backlit crucifix behind the choir. It was, then and even in my memory of it now, altogether dreamlike.

I'd been really active in the church all through high school – a member of the Methodist Youth Fellowship, member of the choir, youth delegate to the National Conference on Missions – just the whole thing. But the best was being a member of the choir. We had maroon robes and the processional on Sunday mornings was always quite stirring, as we marched in:

"*For the beauty of the earth,*
For the glory of the skies.

For the love which from our birth
Over and around us lies.
Lord of all, to Thee we raise
This our hymn of grateful praise."

It's still so very clear in my memory, all these years later.

On that specific Christmas, I truly wanted once again to sing with the choir. I knew all the music as well as anyone in the choir did. I could sing all of the tenor parts to the selections from "The Messiah" from memory.

So I asked the choir director, Vince Dodge – who, you may recall, had been the principal of Roosevelt Elementary when I was a kid – if I could participate that day. I told him how much it would mean to me to be able to do that. He knew me well, knew that my music skills were in good shape, and knew I could more than handle the load without needing to practice. He also knew the situation, and knew that I would be returning to Viet Nam within a matter of days. He agreed.

So I went to the choir room and put on the robe. Several members of the choir recognized me and said hello. I didn't notice the chill in the air at the time, though. Probably too caught up in the occasion to feel it.

I remember the processional – the way that the choir walked in step, slightly swaying from side to side as we came in from the front door, down the central aisle, then divided into two – right and left – and went around the altar and up into the choir loft. Somewhere deep in memory, I can smell the scent of the pine boughs through the sanctuary.

It was a good choir – a *really* good choir! It was not unusual for it to be accompanied by small orchestral groups, backed up by an organist of concert-quality talent. The music was, as "The Messiah" inevitably is, exalting. It was the music that, more than anything else, gave me a sense that Just Perhaps the idea of a God isn't all that far-fetched.

It was wonderful!

The Christmas message was the same timeless message as always. Same scriptures, same lessons, essentially the same sermon – save that the pastor mentioned that the congregation ought to remember those fighting in its name in Viet Nam. No political message – just a reminder.

The recessional leaving the service was the same. That sense of Belonging to something larger than yourself, some sort of congregation with the same beliefs. It was so very meaningful to do that once again. However briefly, it re-established contact between my life as I was experiencing it at the time, and the larger context of contact with others in the real world.

Returning to the choir room, it all fell apart.

Apparently several of the choir members were *most* put out that I had been allowed to sing with them. I'm sure, to this day, that the remarks made were in that special tone of voice that I was meant to hear, even though ostensibly they were supposed to be private. I remember two of The Ladies saying that They Would Discuss This with Vince, and tell him that if he was going to accept strangers into the choir, that they were not going to bother with being members and coming to the rehearsals if that's all it meant. Several other members agreed, also in semi-hushed tones, that allowing such a thing was entirely improper, and how dare someone ask to be in the choir who was not a member.

"For the love which from our birth
Over and around us lies...."

It burned! It hurt – deeply. I apologized to Vince for my intrusion, and assured him that I certainly had no intention of bothering anyone. He allowed as that perhaps he'd made an

154

error at that, and said he'd explain it to the choir members and that in the future there would be a policy on such a request.

I left the church that day. Not just the Methodist Church – I left the church altogether. I've not returned since, save out of respect to others in weddings and funerals. I discovered that the high-sounding words really are meaningless in so many ways, and that the church functioned more as a social entity than a means of doing what it said it did.

Frankly, across 37 years, I haven't missed it. I try to live a moral life, and mostly I do. I remain connected to my community, do good things, follow the teachings of the 25th chapter of Matthew as well as I can. My wife and I informed our families a decade ago that if they didn't now have the Stuff they wanted, it was because they simply didn't bother to buy it. We were going to spend what we had previously spent on Stuff by donating to various charities in the community that actually did do some hands-on work with "the least of these" among us. We continue to do that. My family gets homemade jam and pickles, and that probably has more meaning than the latest electronic gizmo. All in all, the fellowship of a congregation has been neither necessary nor important. She's a recovering catholic. I'm a recovering fundamentalist (came from a family where both of my parents were ordained in the sect).

By their acts shall ye know them. Seems fair.

In writing this, I offer no new epiphany of self-realization that at long last the lost sheep will return to the fold and rejoin the ninety-and-nine once again. That got burned out of me 37 years ago. It didn't send me into a tailspin, it didn't cause PTSD, I didn't take up drugs or alcohol, and I didn't hate the church.

It just made me Indifferent.

Which is, perhaps, a far worse outcome than bitterness or hatred.

The bright side to it was the realization that a good and moral and involved life could be lived without the fellowship and involvement of a church – no matter how open-minded (I've seen the television ads) it claims to be any more.

In so many ways, it simply doesn't matter. I doubt it ever can or will again, in the same way. I no longer even feel a twinge of regret about it. I thought maybe I would, but I don't.

I have no lesson to take from all of this. What's done is done, and we cannot enter the same river twice. I have no lesson to suggest, other than the obvious thing about human compassion maybe being more important than choir membership.

I don't know what churches are doing for those from the current spate of wars. I don't follow those things any more. I do know that much of the "re-integration" of soldiers back into their home communities requires a deeper sort of human compassion than apparently happens. But that's not my issue.

The future is always open for discussion. I offer no hope and no promise of future involvement.

Whatever connection to the divine I require, I have long since found ways to accommodate.

But the memory abides.

30.

The Extended Tour

"We gotta get outta this place!
If it's the last thing we ever do..."

I returned to Viet Nam in mid-January, 1968. It was a time of considerable unpleasantness. Luck was about to run out, my life and duties were about to change. Going home for Christmas had seemed like a wise choice and a good thing at the time. Going back was not.

I returned to Vietnam in January, 1968, just in time for the start of the Tet Offensive. Wikipedia describes the Tet Offensive as "one of the largest military campaigns" of the war, "a series of surprise attacks... throughout South Vietnam... launched in the late night hours of 30 January..."

What had been a mostly uneventful tour became far more dangerous, because Phu Loi – the U.S. Army Airfield where I'd been snatched up by Vic Barry to clerk and play cards for the better part of 1967, and to where I returned after Christmas – was located at the southern tip of what was then known as the Iron Triangle. It rapidly became the site of numerous rocket and mortar attacks, several full-on attacks by North Vietnamese regulars, and the entire area around it became the scene of numerous battles large and small.

After the first part of the Tet Offensive, which was pretty much over by mid-March, my assigned duties became more focused on the war side of things. I was appointed to lead a group of about 25 people – I called them my Combat Clerks – to be prepared for any future attacks on Phu Loi, and I was involved more directly in direct actions on the line than during all of 1967.

It wasn't so much that I changed. The nature of the war itself changed – dramatically.

At the same time, there was all the other stuff going on back home. Martin Luther King and Bobby Kennedy were both killed, LBJ took himself out of that year's election, and the entire stance of the U.S. military in Viet Nam was under review. Walter Cronkite, anchor of the CBS Evening News, and by Gallup Poll "The Most Trusted Man in America," said he could no longer support the mission (though he always continued to support the soldiers ordered to carry it out). The rest of the nation collectively began to decide that it was time to bring things to a close and leave.

Cronkite was right. In late 1967, The Idiot Westmoreland – I call him that because after all these years I've concluded that though he certainly Looked the part of a U.S. General, he was demonstrably inept on the field, with a clear disregard for the lives of those under his command – Westmoreland toured the U.S. telling people that the North Vietnamese and Viet Cong were no longer capable of launching large-scale attacks on U.S. or South Vietnamese forces. Vo Nguyen Giap, the North Vietnamese commander, soon proved him wrong.

In South Viet Nam, the enlisted personnel would gather around the juke boxes in clubs to play popular songs of the era. One of their favorites was by the Animals, with the lyrics:

We gotta get out of this place!
If it's the last thing we ever do...

This song was sung along to with great enthusiasm. The enlisted personnel knew. It was just that everybody else didn't.

I just do Not want even to start with war stories. Just don't. I've always felt uncomfortable doing that. I did get into combat, and more than once. There's a small story in a September, 1968 issue of the Fargo Forum on one of the inside pages where I'm mentioned on my return from home. I went there in January of 1967 as a Private E2 and was a SGT E5 by March of 1968.

While I was there, I read - a Lot. My favorite was the Ring Trilogy, by JRR Tolkien. It always felt as though the adventures of Bilbo and Frodo and Gandalf were somehow more real than the things going on around me daily. I also listened to a lot of Beatles.

I was awarded the Bronze Star for Heroism in Ground Combat for actions of 17-18 February 1968, which I received at a ceremony sometime in August, shortly before I rotated home, out of both the war and the Army. I was delighted to be finished with it.

I didn't and don't have PTSD. I wasn't affected by Agent Orange. I didn't develop a drug habit – didn't take any at all, in fact. Just didn't seem like a good idea. I didn't drink too much, like the other NCO's did, more than they should. I was always conscious that at some point, I was going to leave Viet Nam and try to return to a more normal life.

I think that captures some of the larger issues. The smaller more personal ones are mine – and there are days when either revisiting them is to come too close to it all again, or to remind me of six names on The Wall that reopen too much sadness and grief.

I just don't want to go there any more, even after 45 years.

That is not to say that the war didn't change me. It did. I don't exactly understand how, more than 45 years later. Sometimes it's as though when I think of my life before Viet Nam and revisit it afterwards, it's as though I'm really remembering a movie about someone else. But I can't put my finger on precisely why that is, or why it should be like that.

The world as I knew it had also changed – no question. But I had changed too – even more. Re-entering life in Fargo was a challenge. Just was.

I do know I came back angry at having that part of my own life wasted to no particular purpose. I remember sitting listening to music, especially a song by Glenn Yarbrough titled *Everybody's Wrong*:

> *Listen to my song, it isn't very long.*
> *You'll see before I'm gone, everybody's wrong.*
> *Those of us who run to catch a moment in the sun*
> *Seemed to find when we're done*
> *We weren't supposed to run.*
> *And there's too many words going down.*
> *They keep ringing against the wall with a hollow sound.*
> *All about how it's gonna be*
> *Yes, you'll know what it was – you'll see.*
> *It ain't paying you and me – not a crown.*
> *Finding what you sought*
> *After all the time you fought*
> *Sometimes leaves you with the thought...*
> *Perhaps you've just been bought.*

160

That just now came to me as I wrote this, and it's been years since I've heard it. Apparently it made more of an impression than I realized.

It took several months for the anger to dissipate. I may have simply hidden some of it under a veil of either humor or public indifference.

"Xin Loi," as the Vietnamese and US troops used to say. "Sorry about that."

"It don't mean nuthin!"

We said that too.

31.

When Donnie Came Marching Home

August 23, 1968

I was "outprocessed" at Ft. Lewis, Washington. Having made a Lot of money playing poker and side-betting the dice tables while in Viet Nam, I was flush. Most of which I kept in a Chase Manhattan Bank, Saigon Branch, checking account. I had a taxi standing by to take me to Sea-Tac – in the military I'd gotten used to referring to things by their official abbreviations, and Sea-Tac was the official abbreviation for the Seattle-Tacoma Airport.

At Sea-Tac, there was a long line of other soldiers flying Military Standby. When I got there, one of them called out, "The line starts here, Sarge."   I responded, "I have reservations." And kept right on going. I had First Class reservations, in fact. I could afford it.   (This was well before the airlines would automatically upgrade soldiers obviously returning from overseas to First Class if there was any room. I paid for my own.)

I slept from Sea-Tac to Minneapolis. Short layover – I recall getting a shoeshine and, for the last time in my life, an actual shave at a barbershop. Got on the plane to Hector Field and arrived in Fargo sometime in mid-Afternoon.

Somewhere around here I have a slide of my family waiting for me at the gate. There were no jetways so it was a genuine gate. It's not a very good picture – taken through the window of the airplane. I do recall that my sister Lois had brought her rabbit along.

Mom had tears. I think I did too.

I was home! It had been a Very long two years. I was also out of the Army completely. My two-year enlistment was over, I had no further reserve duty and that was the end of it.

That first night, I was asleep when some idiot coming by tossed some sort of firework out of a car, and I awoke hollering "Incoming" and trying to burrow under the bed. My stepfather came downstairs wondering what I was fussing about, or to see if everything was all right. It was. Took me several hours to get back to sleep.

I'd been released three weeks or so early – an "early out" – so I could go back to NDSU once again in the Fall Quarter. The Army seems to have concluded that having SGT Homuth remain in Viet Nam until after school started probably would not win the war. Besides, I'd been there twenty months, and that was more than enough. So my first day back I wandered out to the campus, sought the registrar, got the registration process properly underway, and looked up several old friends.

There was no overt Negative reaction. No one called me anything bad. Several had No Idea I'd been gone at all, in fact. Some knew, but chose to say nothing. The ones who tried to say something didn't know how – there was no point of contact between my recent experience and theirs out here in The World. That left us with little to talk about.

One old friend's Dad, though, had once been a Scoutmaster to the troop of Boy Scouts I had been in some years earlier. So

163

when I went to my friend's house, there was his Dad. He was Just Delighted to see me.

"Well, Don," he said with a huge Rotary Club grin and some obviously genuine pleasure. "I heard you were in Viet Nam, and it's Great to see you home again." That was nice – he meant it. Truth be told, he thought I was a huge pain in the ass when I was in Scouts – and I was. But those times were now years back.

He was a World War II vet. Quite proud of it, in fact. Made a Big Deal out of it whenever he had a chance. He was active in the local American Legion Club, just off Broadway on Second Avenue. You must remember that at this point, most of the World War II vets were just approaching middle age. The average age of U.S. soldiers in World War II was 26, and this was 23 years later. They were in their late 40s or early 50s, and by then running the show pretty much nationwide.

"I'd like you to do something for me," he said. "I'd like you to put on your Class A uniform (the green one with the tie) and all your medals and come down to the Legion tomorrow. I want to show you off to some friends."

Hey – he had been my Scoutmaster. Seemed like a reasonable enough request. So next day, I stood very close to the razor, put on the greens, made sure the badges were all where they should be and joined him there. There were maybe two dozen at the bar, all with drinks. It was maybe three in the afternoon. The place was full of smoke.

He was proud. Genuinely proud – of that I'm sure. He introduced me all around, and the Greatest Generation shook my hand and offered to buy me drinks. Plural. No thanks – drinking in the afternoon has never been one of my preferences. Probably came from my upbringing in the Salvation Army. I would drink, now and again, but Lord – not at that hour of the day.

The boys at the bar were pretty well liquored up. I could tell that from their voices and faces. I felt uncomfortable. And then it started...

At first, the things they said were all about wanting to hear some War Stories. I didn't have anything I wanted to share with them. They wanted to hear about my Bronze Star – the one for Heroism, not the other more common one. I told them I earned it during the Tet Offensive, but beyond that I simply didn't feel like getting into that sort of thing with people I really didn't know. Then they got into it...

To hear them talk about their exploits, each and every one of them had climbed Mt. Suribachi, or was at Bastogne or in Normandy on D-Day or something equally wonderful and heroic. We didn't know how good we had it because we were only there for a year while They were drafted/enlisted for the Duration. We got to ride around in helicopters while They had to march twenty miles there and back, uphill in the snow, both ways.

And on and On and On and on and on....

Problem was, I knew something important. In World War II, Maybe one soldier in twelve or so ever got close enough to the action to hear a shot being fired, much less participate. The rest were in support – well behind the lines. So it couldn't be the case that each one of these worthies had done what he was claiming.

And then it got Real pointed....

We – the Americans – just didn't fight hard enough. We didn't have Patton. (That's true enough, but we had the idiot Westmoreland who wanted to be Patton, and never could figure out why Vo Nguyen Giap simply out-generalled him at every turn.) Since we had plentiful supplies and good transport, we were not as battle-hardened as They had been. And we weren't fighting the Germans or the Japanese. Now They were really

165

Good soldiers, and the VC and NVA – Viet Cong and North Vietnamese Army – just weren't of the same stuff.

And by God, They knew how to fight, and if They were in Viet Nam, why the war would be over in a week

I had this moment of realization. These people wanted to blame the way the war was conducted on me and my fellow soldiers. I was dumbfounded! I didn't show it, but they had No idea how deeply offensive their talk was. Oh, I know the booze drove some of it. I know that some of them probably had memories of their own they had difficulty coming to terms with. But at the time, they were talking to Me. Personally. And I was having None of it. Criticizing someone else's conduct in a war that You were not in was at best unmannerly. There are better descriptions. I won't use them.

After maybe an hour and a half, it was time to leave. I had to meet someone at 5 p.m. and needed to get out of the Class A's and into Person clothes. I made my excuse, and my Scoutmaster walked me to the door.

"So, Don – When can we sign you up and get you an American Legion card?"

I had to say Something – the insult had, to that point, been almost enough to set me off, and you Know how crazy we Viet Nam veterans can get. Just the littlest thing is enough to put us into a rage, right? (Nah. I wouldn't have done that. I came home OK. I knew several who had not.)

So I looked him straight in the eye and said, "When hell freezes over."

He was shocked – had No idea of what had been happening He stammered a bit, and asked me why.

"You go back and tell those Hero friends of yours that the way this war is being fought is not Our fault. Tell them they may claim whatever they want, but I know better. But most of all, tell them Never to badmouth another Viet Nam vet, Ever."

(I have never joined the American Legion, for just that reason. I promised myself that day never to join, and I never will. I know – most of them are now dead. I don't really care.)

I didn't wait for an answer. I spun on my heel and left. Some weeks later he and I crossed paths again, and he tried to apologize. I told him he had done nothing to apologize for – that so far as I was concerned, we were still on good terms and would remain friends. Our relationship thereafter was slightly strained, but still polite and congenial. He died several years ago. I felt bad to hear the news.

All this stuff about the Greatest Generation has, since then, never rung quite true to me. No question, they did indeed save the world. We weren't asked or tasked to save the world – those who sent us into battle had a different sort of agenda entirely. We just went where we were sent.

But there is something else.

When it came time for them to pass legislation (the World War II vets then ran Congress and most State Legislatures) that would provide the same GI Bill Benefits to returning VietVets as they had received at the end of World War II, they chose not to do that. The Vietnam-era GI Bill of Rights never came close to the earlier version. The ND State Legislature passed a bill providing a cash bonus, but the bonus was reduced if you accepted a state scholarship back to college.

There was a fellow in Congress, Chair of the House Veterans Committee, named Sonny Montgomery. He sponsored the GI Bill of Rights. I once ran across him in DC and asked him why his bill wasn't as generous as the World War II bill. In a moment of candor, he simply said, "They won their war."

He was an early opponent of VA involvement with the entire Agent Orange set of problems, and waited years till he started to support it. Meanwhile, my late brother died from AO complications. Better late, perhaps – but not that much better. Sonny now has several federal buildings named after him.

The Vietnam Veterans of America has, as its founding motto, this: *Never again will one generation of veterans abandon another.*

There's a reason for that. Now you may know why. I always felt More rejected by those World War II vets at the Fargo American Legion than by any of the protesting students I met afterwards at NDSU.

Is it anger? No – it may once have been, but that's long since dissipated into the passage of time. But it is Memory – and not all memories from Fargo were always good.

32.

Bright College Days

A little of the insider story of how the Zip to Zap happened.
"....oh carefree days gone by...." Tom Lehrer
Well, no – not quite.

After twenty months in Viet Nam, coming back to Fargo and to NDSU was more of a transition than I had anticipated. I was aware that some returnees had problems, but had convinced myself that I was somehow above all that, and could handle things pretty well all on my own.

At NDSU, I registered as a History major. A far piece from the Botany major I'd started out as five years before. I recall thinking at the time that there just Had to be a good reason for all the nonsense I'd just been involved with, and perhaps a study of History would help me to understand what it was all about. I registered for some classes with Yur Bok Lee, a Korean professor, about Japanese history specifically and Asian history generally and started to settle back into college life once again.

And nearly flunked out of the Fall quarter.

I'm not a bad student. I have good study habits. I can read fairly quickly and comprehend most of what I read reasonably well. But I recall sitting in those classes listening to lectures, and my mind would wander off elsewhere, often to the previous months in Viet Nam. They weren't Flashbacks – it wasn't as though I was re-living those experiences. They were more like watching a movie – a sense that what I was thinking about happened to someone other than me. To some extent, that's still true now, some 45 years later.

It was a wasted quarter, altogether. Nothing I read stuck with me, the things I tried to write were mostly inchoate. Linear thinking, which I had prided myself was a sort of specialty for me, simply was too hard to deal with. I probably should have sat it out for a quarter, but part of the reason I managed to leave Viet Nam was because I got an "early out" of about 3-4 weeks. That was a deal with the Army where if a person was scheduled to leave (or as we called it at the time DEROS – the Date of Estimated Return from Overseas Service) and was registered to enter an education program, the Army would allow them to return earlier, in time to attend classes.

I was due to leave officially as of mid/late September. By registering for classes, I got to leave in late August. So I was stuck. I just Had to go back to school.

No – I didn't get depressed about the problem. I didn't get into drugs – I was afraid of them. I didn't do booze – simply didn't care for it all that much. I didn't get violent – had enough of that already. Mostly I didn't do much of anything, and even now don't recall it all that well.

But there was one class I signed up for that really did change my life – much for the better. I took a Speech class from E. James Ubbelohde. EJ, as he was known, was a most remarkable teacher. He radiated an air of empathy, and over the quarter he and I chatted many times in his office about what it was to be a returning veteran from a continuing war. No – I never once made that into the subject of a speech in class. The events were still too close in time for that.

170

But I did change my major to Speech, and thrived at it thereafter. I became involved in intercollegiate forensics activities once again, just as I had before I joined the Army. I also took a bunch of writing classes, from really good instructors. It was reasonably clear that even though NDSU didn't then offer a Communications major, nevertheless that's what I was really most competent at. It wasn't so much what I wanted to Be any more – it was more about dealing with who I really was.

So that went well.

In addition, I re-involved myself with the YMCA of NDSU, then being run by Russ Meyer. It had moved from a room in Ceres Hall to a smallish house over on College Street, I believe, near the campus. It had become a sort of focal point for what passed (this was NDSU, after all, not Berkeley) as the Radical group on campus.

I was then nearly 25 years old, and most of these kids were 18 or 19. I thought they were mostly just mildly amusing. There was a smallish chapter of the SDS (Students for a Democratic Society) locally. The SDS was considered, at the time, one of those College Student Radical Groups in most places, and these North Dakota kids were doing their very best to live up to that image. It just wasn't in them. As campus radicals, they were more amusing than dangerous. But all in all nice kids anyway. They chose the name for their group the "Up Against The Wheatfields MF" chapter of the SDS. (Yeah – that's what the MF stood for, but they didn't dare actually say it. See what I mean?)

They apparently thought I was a Narc.

As in a Narcotics Officer sent among them by The Man to find drug use and report it to the authorities. Really – they did think that. I wasn't. I knew that's what they thought, though, and I thought that was pretty funny.

171

I was certainly more conservative politically than most of them were, and made a good deal of fun out of their endless philosophical discussions concerning matters about which they had mostly No comprehension. But I never really joined the group. I didn't go to their parties – I wasn't invited. I didn't go to their meetings – I mostly didn't care.

I did become Highly amused when The Spectrum, the student newspaper, found itself enmeshed in the then-nationwide and highly popular Dirty Word Controversy. In the case of The Spectrum, it began when one of the SDS members wrote a Letter to the Editor, in which he used the phrase "Bullshit is in the eye of the beholder."

Now come On here! As dirty words go, this was even then pretty tame stuff. I'm quite certain that most of the farm kids attending the school had heard the term since they were small children. Doubtless their fathers had used it too – it's a useful descriptor. No question in my mind, they'd heard it from their fellow students on the campus many times over. But...to actually See it in print??? The mind, the sensibilities and the entire Sense of Social Propriety were deeply offended by that, and the controversy ensued.

That got completely and entirely out of hand, when the matter hit the State Senate in the 1969 session. State Senator Richard Forkner (interesting fellow – we were to meet later under quite different circumstances) submitted a bill into the Senate to ban the printing of dirty words in campus newspapers. No – he didn't use George Carlin's list – more's the pity. He couched it in more vague language having to do with Profanity or Crude language or something along that line.

Then the Fates intervened, as they sometimes will, in some highly propitious and quite funny ways. When a bill is submitted into the legislature, unless a special request is made for a specific number – like the main appropriations bill is

172

usually HB1 for example – the numbers are assigned on a first come basis. That was the case this time.

It came out as Senate Bill 69.

No – I am Not kidding about this. That's what it was. No one could have asked for a better number. I thought it was hilarious, as did most of those who could discern the significance of the number. (In all candor, not everyone could. It was too much effort to explain it to those who couldn't.)

By that time, I was writing an Op-Ed column for The Spectrum not exactly in opposition to the main editorial slant, but mainly to provide a more moderate contrast to some of the philosophy expressed by then-editor Kevin Carvell – himself an Army, though not a Viet Nam, veteran. He was, at most, mildly but not excessively radical-left, and I considered myself more of a Moderate Extremist.

I couldn't resist the temptation. In every instance thereafter, I referred to Forkner's SB 69 as "The Bill That Dare Not Speak Its Name" and had no end of fun ridiculing it fiercely. It didn't pass. Just as well, because we were prepared to ignore it and raise a fuss over censorship had it done so.

Kevin – who later became Senator Byron Dorgan's district aide through pretty much his entire career – burned out and decided to go sit out by Mott, North Dakota and get his head straight. Or something. Anyway, he announced his resignation, and the Board of Student Publications had to pick a new editor in Spring of 1969. I applied, and got the job.

In his final act as editor, Kevin wrote a tongue-in-cheek piece, which ran at the bottom of the front page of the paper. Then he left town. The piece was about having the NDSU students go to Zap, a small town in central North Dakota, on Spring Break. Kevin called it "Zip to Zap." It was meant to be a send-up of the usual Spring Break in Ft. Lauderdale, Florida and as a satire, it was hugely funny. Several of us said we actually might Zip to Zap. We could drive to Bismarck, stay overnight with some friends, then go to Zap, cook some hot dogs and drink a few beers in the park, be able to say we had Zipped to Zap and go home.

Really, that was all it was ever meant to be. At first.

Then things started to get all out of hand – with a vengeance.

First, the NDSU Veterans Club said they wanted to go, too. Well, why not? What's another half dozen or so? They apparently told the UND Veterans Club up in Grand Forks about it, and then they called and said they wanted to go, too. So even at that, maybe two dozen people or so – no big deal.

At which point, the dam broke. A local AP reporter/stringer (I've forgotten his name) put the story on the ND wire. Look at these college kids – going to Zip to Zap. Isn't that funny?

Not for long, it wasn't. The story made the A wire, and pandemonium ensued. It was printed all over the nation, and immediately the phone on my desk began to ring.

Non-stop.

Someone from the U of Minnesota wanted to come up. Would that be OK? Sure! I had no authority to stop them. Another from the South Dakota School of Mines. Then a call from Illinois. And Florida! (Florida? Why would They want to do that? Ft. Lauderdale was *theirs*. I was in no position to say No, regardless.) It just kept growing and growing, doubling in size nearly every day for a week, anyway.

The local television stations wanted to do an interview. Kevin was not available – I think he'd gone to Mott – so I was it. The WDAY crew wanted me to pose near a Beatles poster about "We could change the world, if they only knew." I wouldn't do that – this had Nothing to do with the Student Movement, as it was called at the time. It was then still mostly not that big a deal.

But it got bigger still.

Eventually the Mayor of Zap called – Norman Fuchs (pronounced fyooks). A very nice man, he was somewhat taken aback by all of this, but was game to have a good go at an enjoyable weekend. He inquired what sorts of numbers he could expect, and I told him that nearly as I could tell – and I certainly didn't have all the information because I wasn't really coordinating anything – somewhere around maybe three thousand.

You could hear his teeth drop over the phone, I swear. Zap had a total population of maybe 300.

He said he'd get back to me the next day, and he did. He had contacted some local people to work on setting up a proper reception. The local Cow Belles (a livestock ladies group) were going to sell fleischkuchle. An unused bar was leased and would be reopened for the weekend by someone from Dickinson. I told him that several bands had said they wanted to play gratis. He said he'd work on getting a stage with some power to it.

And it grew and grew. Nobody knew for certain what was going to happen. It was, in the parlance of the time, a Happening.

The event, however, had not gone unnoticed. The Governor, Bill Guy, called in the State Police folks and the ND National Guard to discuss what to do with this massive influx of crazed young people. Who Knows what sort of mayhem could result without proper authoritarian guidance? So they put together some plans, and implemented riot control training, and arranged to deploy their forces into the field (quite literally in this case – Zap is just a no-stoplight town surrounded by fields) to deal with what they were quite certain would happen. There were, apparently, no plans just to leave things be and let well enough alone.

175

The kids came in droves. And they drank beer – a Lot of beer. In order to control the amount of beer drunk, the bars started to raise their prices arbitrarily. That would, they surmised, mean two things – higher profit and less consumption. They didn't reckon that all it would do was make the students angry.

It was cold that night. A building nearby had previously been torn down and a pile of scrap wood left. Several members of the two Veterans' Clubs built a smallish fire to warm themselves by. It didn't stay small for long – it got quite large. But it was in the middle of a large intersection, and wasn't any real danger to any nearby structure.

The vets, though, were by this time pretty well hammered. Several of them peed into the fire – to the general consternation of the law enforcement types detailed to observe the proceedings.

Mayor Fuchs, meanwhile, was encamped on a nearby hillside with the National Guard commander and State Police commander on the scene. He could see the bonfire flames from a distance, and had no real sense of what was really going on. The NG and SP commanders kept saying "Any time you want, Mayor – we'll just move in there and get those students out!" He told me later they must have said this two dozen times, and it finally wore him down till he said OK.

It takes time to move anti-riot troops into position. Hours, in fact. By the time they were ready to go, all the fuss had ended. The bonfire had died down to nothing, and the kids were mostly sleeping (it off in some cases) in their tents in the fields.

But the order had been given, the troops deployed and the command was given to Move Them Out. They started just before dawn.

A good many of the NG types were students at NDSU or UND, and if they'd had their way they'd have been participants, not doing riot control. As they went through the tents, they listened carefully to hear whether or not there might be a couple in there maybe having (ahem – a little discretion here) "relations" at that hour. When, as several of them told me later, they found someone doing that, they'd put four troops around the tent quietly, grab the corners and lift it up, yelling "Surprise!" to the doubtless startled couple therein.

North Dakota Riot Control.

While there was excellent planning for the event, there was No planning given to orderly traffic control in the event of a rapid evacuation of the area. Cars went every which way, sometimes having minor collisions with each other. It was motorized pandemonium!

This was being carried – Live! – by KFYR radio in Bismarck, who had a reporter in a helicopter with state officials, and was breathlessly reporting on the way the kids were fleeing in convoys down nearby roads, being Hotly Pursued by the National Guard vehicles.

Now stop and think just for a minute. Here are the students in normal vehicles, being chased by jeeps and deuce-and-a-halfs. There was No way the NG vehicles would ever catch them, and what would they do if they had? It was all Most strange!

In their panic to leave, the students threw beer by the can, six-pack and even cases into the ditches nearby so as not to be caught with it later. A wise precaution.

Some of them got to Hazen. An NDSU student, whose father was a local banker, was on the top of the bank tossing cans of beer down to a smallish crowd on the street. The NG troops lined up with bayonets fixed, and marched resolutely toward the students. When one didn't move quite quickly enough, he got stabbed. In the butt!

Locals tell the story, and it's probably true, how a local doctor (or it might have been a veterinarian – the story varies) sewed the gash up without anesthetics.

Eventually many of the kids ended up camping the next day in the park in Bismarck. Bismarckers duly got into their cars with their kids and drove white-knuckled through the park in a disapproving parade just to look at Those Students. Those Students, meanwhile, were flanging on their guitars and hanging out, waving at those coming by.

It all ended with pretty much nothing. Those en route to Zap got the word, turned around and went home. The Cow Belles lost money. Those who leased the closed bar may have made money – no one ever heard, or at least bothered to say.

The press reaction was worldwide and wonderful. The best was from Pravda – the official mouthpiece of the Soviet Union. Its report concluded that a bunch of overprivileged bourgeoisie American students had descended on a small coal-mining town full of proletariat workers, and had essentially destroyed it.

That myth, or something like it, seemed to get picked up by some American press. It wasn't a urban legend. It was a rural one. Several newspapers reported that the students had torn down a building and burned it. Nope – that didn't happen.

Overall, the damage was slight. The student government and The Spectrum pledged ten thousand dollars to indemnify any damage claims that could be substantiated. All we ever heard about was a cracked window and damage to a small section of picket fence. Other than that, nothing.

It ended up with most, particularly those in power, being hugely embarrassed and abashed by the whole thing. People put it out of their minds, determined Never to discuss it ever again, and went about their lives.

178

There was a smallish rumor about staging another event in 1970, in the nearby Minnesota town of Climax. Like the Zip to Zap, this would be called the Come to Climax.

Nothing ever came of it.

The national interest generally, and the Student Movement specifically, were about to change dramatically, and not for the better. Viet Nam War protests were about to become larger and occasionally more violent. Kent State wasn't far off.

In 2009, the City of Zap held a 40th reunion, and a couple of hundred people showed up. That included both the students and the National Guard types. It was a pleasant enough day – and everyone there had a good time telling and re-telling the stories of what had happened in May of 1969. I enjoyed it immensely. I was sad to hear that Mayor Fuchs died some time back. I'd liked to have seen him again.

After the original Zip, I learned, the nearby high school kids patrolled all the ditches for miles around. They managed to collect enough beer to last them well into the summer of '69.

33.

Pranks for the Memories

It still brings a smile whenever I think of it.

The cannon – a World War II artillery piece if memory serves – in front of the Old Field House (which was then just the Field House) on NDSU was an annual target to be painted. Some years it was polka dots, some years it was candy striped, some years the barrel was pink. It wasn't terribly creative – it was just something that happened every year.

But it was way too obvious to be a really good prank.

The immediate response would come the next morning, when the Army ROTC cadre would show up (they were located in the Field House), see the painting and immediately that morning repaint it olive drab with what seemed to be an endless supply of the stuff kept for just such emergencies. I suspect that cannon probably had annular paint rings on the barrel – one for each year it was there and repainted – much like the annular growth rings inside the trunks of trees.

As pranks went, such visible painting was Far too obvious. A good prank required something more subtle – something that had staying power and would last longer. Something we could see for several days and point out to friends, thereby to gain bragging rights to creative prankery.

We came up with the nearly Perfect prank:

One night, several friends of mine and I painted whitewalls on the tires.

Simple really. Whitewalls were Not Obvious, but anyone actually Seeing it (which is somewhat different from just looking at it) might catch on. Or maybe not.

In this case, not.

It wasn't noticed for ten days or so. The cannon just sat there, with whitewalls.

I suspect someone finally pointed it out to the ROTC people, who painted the whitewalls over straightaway. But there, for a while, the NDSU cannon had whitewalls.

That, my friends, is Subtle Prankery writ large. There were other pranks over the years, but that may well have been The Best Prank I pulled in my entire life. Just because it was So subtle.

It still brings a smile whenever I think of it.

Been years since I've done a good prank. No good targets, no friends close enough to see the humor in it, so no point. Any more, if friends and I happen to think of a good prank, we just tell each other about it, but never actually Do it.

As trenchant a comment on Aging as there is, I guess.

34.

Somethin' Happenin' Here

...What it is ain't exactly clear.

It was an odd time. Opposition to the Viet Nam War and the draft was growing across the nation. The Chicago Democratic Convention of 1968 was still fresh in folks' minds. The impact of it was yet to be fully felt. The Kent State Massacre was well into the future. John Kerry's testimony about the war was two years off. But there was Something going on – it was just that nobody knew exactly what.

In Fargo, the local authorities were on guard, but not overly concerned. The three four-year institutions each had a decidedly different sort of student body and environment. Concordia College was, according to conventional wisdom of the time, the place where Minnesota and North Dakota Lutherans sent their daughters to meet nice Lutheran boys to get into the music program – which really was quite good. Moorhead State College, though, was the place that was supposed to be Radical. That was more by reputation than reality. Yeah, some of the students there dressed in strange clothes (and truth be told, it's hard to Dress Radical in a Fargo-Moorhead winter anyway) and let their hair go long (hair was still an issue for some) and every now and again there'd be some sort of half-hearted protest about something or other, but mostly local folks just took them all in stride with an air of bemusement.

NDSU was different from either of those. It was far larger. Though it had a smallish SDS chapter, those in it were singularly ineffective in doing the sort of Student Mobilization that was yet to come and be feared in other places. It also had the "suitcase student" phenomenon – the kids would drive from across the state for the M-F classes, then pack up Friday night and drive back home to spend the weekends in their local towns.

(NDSU actually knew the answer to the old World War I song "How you gonna keep them down on the farm....? A bunch of them never really left!)

The "student radicals" that were gaining notoriety elsewhere – few of whom were actually students, but mostly just hangers-on in far-off exotic places like Berkeley – were getting some press. Now and again a protest would turn violent. People were concerned that It Could Happen Here, right here in Fargo.

Well, no – not really. Certainly not at Concordia. Never there. They may have expressed a sort of Christian Concern about Viet Nam every now and then, but other than some quiet meetings that would be about it. Moorhead State was watched closely. But the students there spent Far more time "getting mellow" than they did plotting action. It just wasn't in them to go quite that far. NDSU was depopulated over the weekends, save for the Greeks who were focusing on resume-building, contact-making (for their later careers), partying and getting laid. Not necessarily in that order.

The student leadership at NDSU made a conscious decision to work collaboratively with the administration in order to ensure that nothing got too far out of hand. The student body president, the late John R. "Butch" Molm, and I would meet regularly with the administration's point person, the late Les

Pavek, the Dean of Students. I always liked Les – from the first time I knew him when he and his wife-to-be taught Phy Ed at Agassiz Junior High School. Les was an affable fellow, deeply sincere and genuinely concerned that the school would function in an orderly manner. So were Butch and I. We were both somewhat older than the student body generally. We had a more vested interest in keeping things calm – which is not Quite the same as Under Control – than in trying to make any political points on a national scale.

There were those in the smallish radical groups who resented that, but we didn't really care. Our assessment was that they weren't going to actually Do anything too terrible, and so long as they were monitored and their activities shunted into Free Expression in a tolerable fashion, we could accommodate them nicely.

There was, though, one more smallish outburst of radical thought. It happened when Abbie Hoffman, one of the famed/dread Chicago Seven, was invited to speak in the old Festival Hall. This attracted the attention of the radicals at MSC and the smallish SDS group at NDSU was just delighted to have him there.

He showed up wearing a Chicago Police Department shirt. Oh – the sheer visual irony of it all! The activists were hugely pleased with that.

As editor of The Spectrum, I had several radical volunteers offering to "report" on the speech. They were young and mostly clueless – I knew full well that what they wanted to do was to get into the polemic of it. I had a policy of sending the "conservatives" to report on the "liberals" and vice versa. If you want to get some sort of "objective" reporting, that's not a bad way to do it.

Abbie was a hoot! He waved his fists, made a bunch of off-the-wall statements about Oppression and Freedom (you hear

184

those now, too, only more often from the opposite side of the political spectrum), pranced around the stage and was hugely entertaining. Content-wise, he really didn't have much to say, but he said it well, loudly and often.

The one statement that came flying out of his spiel was "What this nation needs is fewer mothers, and more mother-fuckers!" Yep – that's what he said, in those exact words, to something like a thousand people right there in Festival Hall. The coterie of radicals cheered loudly – seemingly delighted at the Freedom Of Expression this involved.

But what did it actually Mean? I was sitting in the audience, and I had No idea whatthehell he was trying to say. So far as I could discern, it was altogether content-free with no particular application to anything. (And, after all, what's a Meta for anyways?)

But I knew – I just Knew that the phrase was going to come back to haunt me. And it did. The conservative student reporter, apparently wanting to show how utterly morally bereft Hoffman's presentation was, took great pains to include it as a direct quote in his story. In the normal course of affairs, the story would first be reviewed by the Assistant Editor, Sandy Scheel (later Huseby). She was mildly involved with the radical groups, but not one of the truly shriven. I suspect she believed that I was somehow not to be trusted and far too conservative for her taste.

She brought the story into my office, which was across the hall in the Student Union from the main newsroom, for my review and approval.

"You might want to look at this," she said – with a look on her face that she was expecting me to disapprove of the quote. So I read through it, noted the quote and responded.

"This is what Hoffman actually said. I was there and heard it. So – do You think it needs to be in the story?"

185

"Yes."

"OK. Go with it."

"Are you sure you want to do this? You know what's going to happen."

"What are they going to do? Send me to Viet Nam?" (We used to say that when I was in Viet Nam.)

So we went with it – printed it as quoted and waited for the hue and cry to follow. Which it did in short order.

My response to all of that directly to Laurel Loftsgard, then the NDSU president, and to Les Pavek, was that Hoffman had indeed said Exactly those words, they were heard by a thousand people anyway, and be Damned if I was going to bowdlerize or pretend that he didn't. I also wasn't going to do that asterisk-thing. My job was to ensure that what got into the Spectrum was as accurate as I knew, and that it was the university's job to ensure that its students were subject to accurate statements of fact whenever possible.

I could have lost that skirmish, but didn't. There wasn't a student or faculty on the campus that had not been subjected to the F-bomb in one form or another previously. They weren't exactly virgins. Whatever sense of personal outrage anyone might have experienced was theirs alone, and for them to deal with. I just had to back up my reporters when they did an honest job of reporting. This was.

The best part was the letters from schools around the state. We made it a practice of sending every school library – there used to be school libraries back in those days and they often had actual Newspapers in them for their students to read – a copy of the Spectrum as a way of letting them know the happenings on our campus. Several librarians and principals wrote back Demanding, no less, that we cease sending them any more papers.

186

I told them all – individually – that if they wished to censor what their students could read, they could surely do that on their own. If they wished to cut off all exposure to the altogether more important information for the sake of One word, accurately and properly used, in a report of One story in One issue of the paper, I wouldn't do their work for them or make it any easier.

Unlike the previous Dirty Word controversy, that one blew over rather quickly. No one entered a bill in the legislature to deal with it. I don't recall any great hue and cry from the editorialists around the state. It just went away quietly, save for some minor actions on the campus. Ray Burington, then the staff advisor to The Spectrum, resigned. That was unfortunate – Ray was a genuinely nice man. But he had to report to the administration, whereas I did not. I understood completely. But he didn't have the final say about what got printed. I did. We left it at that.

If there was any great controversy on the campus for me at that time, it was over the Bison football team, and Ron Erhardt, the coach. I took an instant dislike to him first time I met him, and the feeling was mutual. He had coached the team to a Division 2 NCAA national championship, and like many football coaches, he came to believe that he was almost as important as the Alumni Association and Bison Team Makers told him he was.

We got sideways when he demanded about $50K to replace bleachers in the old Field House from the Student Activity Fee. I saw no reason why the students should be paying for seats they would not (and truth be told Could not) use. Bleachers seats aren't activities – they are part of the physical plant. It could come from his budget.

Butch Molm and I and other student leaders had worked hard to get the Student Activity Fee into the control of the Student Senate, rather than solely in the hands of the administration. We figured we knew better what activities students wanted and would pay for than they did.

We came up with the idea of a Student Art Collection, to be funded annually by the Student Activity Fee. Over the years it became quite a good collection of largely regional artists. It even got to the point where the school hired a curator for it, and it had its own place on the upper floor of the Student Union. I have no idea where it eventually went.

The Spectrum also got sideways with Erhardt on another matter more directly involved with the Bison football team. We already had a fascinating reputation – our Wisconsin thugs could defeat most anyone else's Wisconsin thugs. So long as the thugs could play for the team, they were kept on. Once their eligibility was up, they could be expelled from school. One notable player, Paul Hatchett, was a football star, but was gone soon after the team played in its final bowl game his "senior" year.

The NDSU place kicker Jim Twardy got himself into a problem. Seems as how he refused to pay for the services of a whore, and she stabbed him in the stomach with a rat-tail comb. It was a Deep Dark Secret when the team returned. I found out about it less than two days later. My sports guy wrote the story, but we were a weekly paper, and the lag time to publication and release was going to be several days.

Les Pavek called to inquire whether we were going to print it. Yes – I told him – we are indeed. Les said he wished we wouldn't. I told him there was No way a story like that was going to or could be covered up. The Forum didn't have it, and it was a race for The Spectrum to break the story before they did.

Eventually the administration told The Forum. Ed Kolpack was delighted. We carried it two days later. Damn! It would have been fun to scoop The Forum, but the administration couldn't allow that to happen.

Before the end of the school year, I left The Spectrum and went to work for Dewey Heggen at Channel 4 TV. Heggen wanted me to produce a documentary on drug use in Fargo-Moorhead. I wasn't in the drug culture, didn't use them, didn't care to. But I knew some who were, and they knew me, and when I told them I would protect their identities in any filmed interviews. They trusted my word and agreed to discuss it. Few in Fargo-Moorhead were aware that by that time drug use had become as widespread as it was, and it was spreading beyond the colleges down into the high schools. That documentary eventually led me into a full-time job in television.

I was told to graduate in 1970. Yes – the registrar called me up one afternoon and Told me that I had enough credits to graduate, and that I Would be graduating. I hadn't been keeping track – it was a bit of a surprise to me. But it was time.

I had always felt that those traditional graduation gowns and mortar boards were a complete waste of money. Why pay six or seven thousand dollars to some costume firm for a garment that would be worn twice? We could take that money instead and use it to fund scholarships. Butch (the Student Body President) and I pushed it, but met considerable resistance. So it never happened.

In the Letter of Instructions for graduates, the dress code was clear. "Men will wear white shirts, dark ties, dark trousers and shoes" under the black robes. Conformity above all. Not a chance. I wore a gold shirt, purple tie, red shorts, tan Hush Puppy shoes and magenta socks. Friends in the audience told me that as I walked across the stage to get my empty diploma case, every time those socks came out from under the robe, it was like a flash bulb going off.

Laurel Loftsgard saw me coming, and as we shook hands he said, "If anyone was going to wear something like that, it Had to be you." I smiled.

189

I just checked to see if the magenta graduation socks are still where I have stored them for over forty years. They are. They still bring a smile.

35.

Floods, Birds and Soggy Farmers

Folks along the Red River Valley ought to take the time to enjoy those 100-year floods that show up every 3-4 years any more; they bought and paid good money to have them. And for the same reason, the abundant waterfowl of the past will not return, regardless of what Ducks Unlimited tries to do. Simply put, agricultural tiling is yet another 20th century lesson in unintended consequences of which most people in the 21st century remain blissfully ignorant.

It was the flood of '69, a panic in Fargo at the time, and losing one of the north side dikes was a Very near thing! We'd started out merely to do a longish photo feature/story on how NDSU students pitched in to help (just as you may have seen in several of the more recent floods) since The Fargo Forum wasn't doing anything like that, but once we got involved in the actual battle there was no longer much of a chance to take notes and pictures.

We never did get the full feature I had hoped, but that may well have been for the best. The extra two dozen students being right there in the right place at a critical time probably kept at least one of the sandbag barriers from being overtopped.

It was, as I recall it, a Near Thing. Nobody had time to Be A Journalist.

And when it was over, we were exhausted and too damned tired to even write it up. Unfortunate, but OK.

Ahhh! But it ties into a story worth the telling, a story that Should be. Few are aware of it.

Used to be that just beyond Valley City and the west rim of the Red River Valley, the land was full of prairie potholes. Small bodies of water – ponds mostly, and shallow, because the water table was very near the surface most years. Some few still survive near I-94 as you motor west, but back then, if you flew over them, you could see them stretching for miles on a north-south line. Most of them are gone now, but as you fly over you can still see where they used to be, because the soil where they were is darker and their outlines still remain.

Farmers tolerated them, but preferred whenever possible to drain them and put the extra acres into production. Given that many of them had accumulated a layer of fertile muck over the years, doing that was very productive indeed.

It was, if I recall correctly, the USDA that came up with a subsidy to farmers to drain the potholes by laying tile (aka pipes) in the fields. That way when the Spring runoff hit the potholes, the water would leave much faster and flow to the nearest creek, which then led to the river (either the Sheyenne or the James, depending on which side of the divide one was on) and downstream as rapidly as possible. This would then allow the farmers to get into the fields earlier, and in a place where the growing season was short, that was considered an unalloyed Good Thing.

(You may recall the annual Soggy Farmer Story when I worked in television at Channel 4. This is about that.)

Over the years, hundreds and probably thousands of miles of tile were laid in the fields, subsidized by federal Ag funds.

192

Many farmers took advantage of the subsidy, tiled their fields and lo – the tiles worked! Wondrous well, in fact. If you wanted that water Gone, it was Gone.

But....

As the snow melted, the water had to go somewhere, and the more tiles in place, the faster it got to the rivers, rather than being held in the potholes and in the high water tables where it used to collect and flow out more slowly over a period of a couple of months. So the Sheyenne particularly started having problems. That's a Very long river – look at a map – and it drains a Huge watershed. So after all the tiling was done, when the watershed melted, All of that water hit at once, within a period of 10-14 days. With that slug of water going downstream in a streambed that Nature never designed to handle that volume in so short a time, the Sheyenne simply overflowed and the water first sought ditches and then simply flowed overland on its way to the Red.

Had that water been held back even for 10 days, the resulting floods would have been lower. The rivers would have been high but not so dramatically high as they've ended up being. All so the soggy farmers wouldn't be as soggy for as long.

So folks ought to take the time to enjoy these 100-year floods that show up every 3-4 years any more. They bought and paid good money to have them.

And they will continue to have them, because the tiles will remain in place till they plug up, and there will be No government subsidy to remove them.

As an ancillary story, there used to be a Huge waterfowl population on the Great Plains. Ducks and geese and cranes and all sorts of waterfowl. I recall once driving down by Enderlin one Spring day and stopping to look at the sky, which was horizon-to-horizon, north-south-east-west, covered with waterfowl flying north for the annual migration. I stayed parked for more than an hour, and it never stopped. I've asked around and have failed to find anyone who's seen anything like that in many, many years. I still have a vivid auditory memory of the sound that huge flock made as it passed by.

When the potholes were tiled and drained, the habitat disappeared. The waterfowl simultaneously. They will not return regardless of what Ducks Unlimited tries to do. Not without habitat. Ducks and geese don't nest on dry land away from water.

The last twenty years, though, has been a "wet cycle," where North Dakota has had unusual amounts of precipitation most years. Waterfowl numbers have increased dramatically, I'm told.

But no one has seen or heard anything like I saw that day, perhaps thirty years ago, in a very long time.

36.

More Cars and Girls

Well, more cars and a young woman, actually.

The very last day of my special Christmas leave in 1967, I was driving by Muscatell Chevrolet in Fargo when suddenly, I saw a blue second-series Corvair convertible on the lot. I swung in and asked the sales guy on duty how much the Corvair convertible cost.

"Which one?" he asked.

There were two? Indeed, there was the one outside and another inside they'd just taken in. Would I like to look at that one too? Indeed — I would.

It was love at first sight. A 1966 Corsa convertible, black on black with a white top, 4-speed, 4-carb, wire wheel spinner hubcaps, excellent condition. I always thought those cars were stunningly beautiful, so within several hours I put together the deal. The dealership gave a pretty good price — knowing I was going to return to Viet Nam the next morning.

I picked the car up and drove it for maybe 3-4 miles, then to my folks' home and put it in the garage. Where it sat till I got back. While in Viet Nam, I had visions of driving it around when I returned.

On my return, I got it out of the garage. My folks had taken it out and washed it the day before, it had new gas and an oil change. I spent a good part of that first day driving it around with the top down. I recall it well. I went back to college and continued to enjoy it. I soon started dating a very pretty young woman who liked it, too.

But there came a time when my head turned and my attention was caught by a 1966 Corvette roadster with a removable hardtop. I sold the Corvair to the young woman who liked it and bought the Corvette.

In a tale not uncommon to young American men at the time, I married the young woman, so the Corvair was back "in the family" once again.

I learned several Life Lessons:

1. **Corvettes Get Girls!** Well, of Course they do!
2. **Girls know this.** That was Not fully understood.
3. In the fullness of time, **one of those girls will become a Wife**. Wives are not Girls. A subtle difference, but real.

So, after the marriage, the usual "We need a more practical car" discussion occurred, and the Corvette was sold.

PART V

37.

Live at Five

Less than meets the eye.

Newton N. Minow, the former chairman of the Federal Communications Commission, once called commercial television a "vast wasteland." Wise heads nodded in contemplation of the inherent wisdom in that remark, and commercial television just ignored it.

I think that's Far too grandiose a term. It's not Vast at all. It may well not even be Half Vast in small television markets like Fargo. Or at least like Fargo was in the early 1970s, when I worked in it for about three years.

I had come to work for KXJB at the invitation of Dewey Heggen, a much-respected local anchor, to do a one-hour documentary on drug use in the Fargo-Moorhead area. That went pretty well – turns out the local authorities were vaguely aware that there was considerable drug use going on, but had No idea of how much. In my program, I got a bunch of local young people – some in high school – to appear on camera (in silhouette to protect their identities – mostly from their parents) to discuss the relative ease by which they could acquire illegal drugs of various sorts.

As it turned out, there was never any danger that the parents would see it. In fact, there was precious little danger that Anybody would see it. The Channel Four management aired it with No promotion, nothing in the schedule, no on-air promotions at all. Just one Sunday afternoon at four o'clock they stuck the film reel (we still used film, though it was color) on the machines and let it fly.

So much for that whole Community Service requirement in the broadcast license.

Well, no big deal. Heggen liked it, and asked if I would be interested in being a Special Assignments Reporter for the station. I had not thought about that, but absolutely I would. Seemed like an interesting thing to do – something quite out of the ordinary. With my new wife still in school, I needed income, and that would provide a little. As in Very little.

Though viewers may now, as some of them did then, consider being a television personality to be quite glamorous and well-paying, it was not glamorous. It was mostly reporting the same old stuff on a different day. And $700/month was no big deal, even at that time. But it was better than nothing.

I met an interesting fellow at the station – Glenn Scott. He had formerly been a disc jockey on KFGO. Glenn was a fascinating fellow – he had been an English Lit major at MSC, and I suspect he'd read way too much Camus and had fallen into the Existential Dilemma. To some degree, he remains there today – I still consider him one of my best friends.

Glenn had a jaundiced view of The News, which he made clear one afternoon by discussing what comprised a "news" show – which then ran to a half hour at six p.m., right after Walter Cronkite on CBS. First and foremost, in a thirty-minute period, somewhere between 17 and 19 minutes of commercials, depending on local sales. That left 11-13 minutes total for News,

Weather and Sports. The newspaper types would call this the News Hole.

Of the 13 minutes, give up two for banter – the "happy talk" that news anchors are supposed to share with the "news team." That left 11. Of that, take out three for the weather. That left eight minutes. Of that, it would largely depend on whether or not there was a golf tournament for Jim Adelson to report – if there was, he'd get four, usually with a video clip of someone pushing a small white ball on grass toward a hole, and it would either go in or not.

Gripping stuff! (And we haven't even discussed the Farm Markets, which now and again were featured as well. One of these days, I'm going to have to look up just why it was that Barrows and Gilts were always so steady. But good for them anyway – the very idea of Unsteady barrows and gilts is nearly incomprehensible.)*

So the news producer, If he was lucky, would get maybe four minutes to cover The News. That was it – four minutes. Push it to five if there was something Really important going on – but Adelson was a big athletic supporter, and he always wanted more time.

Sometimes I was the standup reporter, sometimes the camera guy. I had been reasonably well prepared for the standup role – my college forensic activities included a bunch of extemporaneous speaking, and I ofttimes could do the whole report in one, at the most two takes with no scripts, cue cards or teleprompter.

Being the camera guy for Adelson, though, occasionally got to be funny. At a local pro-am golf tournament (about half of his on-camera standups), we got to the course, and Jim wandered off to find someone to talk to. I was outside, setting up the gear

---

* barrow: a castrated male domestic pig; gilt: a young female domestic pig.

201

– which was heavy. A nice young man wandered up to me and asked if I wanted to buy tickets for a raffle.

"What's the prize?" I asked.

"A complete set of Wilson clubs and a bag and golf shoes."

"Thanks all the same, but not only do I not Play golf – frankly I don't approve of it." This said in an imperious tone and manner.

I can still see the startled/confused look on his face as he wandered away.

One of the television traditions was that Adelson would interview just about every high school and college coach within the viewing area at the start of the season. I became convinced, through that, that somewhere in the college coaching curriculum, would-be coaches were taught to memorize the Standard Interview. The interviewer would ask a leading question, like "How do you see your team this season?" The answer was a variation on this:

"Well, we lost a bunch of good experienced players this year, but we've got some new kids who have their head on straight. They have a lot of athletic ability. So I think that if we just go out there and Play Our Game (a very important phrase), stick to our game plan, and maybe get a few breaks here and there, why we could be right there in it at the end."

How many times have you heard that same answer or a slight variation of it?

There was also a seasonal component. Come every March or April, it was time to do the Soggy Farmer Story.

North Dakota farmland tends to drain and dry slowly. That heavy lake-bottom clay would stay wet, and defy the best efforts of tractors and plows to do any tilling till it dried. But that had to be caught just right – wait too long to till, the clay would dry and get hard, and that made things bad, too.

So if the Spring Melt came early, we'd do the soggy farmer story in March. If late, we'd do it in April. We'd find a properly soggy farm, find the farmer, put him somewhere with a tractor or an outbuilding in the background, and ask the driving question, "When do you think you'll get into the fields?"

North Dakota farmers are a taciturn bunch, not given to concise answers. We got everything from "maybe next month" to "God only knows." But it was the stuff of News, and so it got on the air.

Glenn and I made our News Director, Howard Schanzer, somewhat nervous to have us around the newsroom. So he'd tell us to "go find a story." While there may well be many stories in the naked city, there weren't always many in the Fargo-Moorhead area. Still and all, we'd cruise around looking for something – anything – that we could film and take back as a 20-30 second Visual for the evening news.

There was that one evening we had turned south onto I-29 just off Main Avenue and there was a horse running down the right-hand side of the Interstate. I have No idea why it was there, where it had been, or where it planned to go. But it was going there quickly. So out came the Bell & Howell camera, and I filmed it as Glenn drove alongside. We followed it down to the I-94 interchange, and it took the interchange and continued at a gallop going West. When it went across both lanes of traffic, across the median, and across both of the other lanes, I momentarily had a sick feeling I was going to be filming a tragedy. But it was a smart horse, it did Not get hit. It ran up the abutment on the other side and disappeared – still going south by west.

We dutifully took the film back to the station, had Paul Froeschle process it, did a little write-up on it which essentially said, "This afternoon at about two-thirty p.m., drivers on I-29 may have been startled to see a horse running along the road. It

203

continued south and turned west onto the side of I-94. It then crossed the road and disappeared. No – there is no information on why it was on the road, or where it was going. We haven't seen or heard of it since."

Neither did anyone else. The horse apparently just disappeared into thin air.

Of such is Local television news made.

There was a better one, though.

One July day after Schanzer told us to go find a story, Glenn and I were at our wit's end trying to come up with Something. We had no clue. So I told Glenn to drive by my house, we'd get a couple of fishing rods and go fishing. Really. If we'd come back with nothing who was going to yell at us?

So we did that – drove over east of Detroit Lakes and went fishing on Lake Seven – or maybe it was Lake Five. I know it wasn't Lake Six, because I often fished there. We rented a boat and I rowed while Glenn fished. I had my trusty Bell & Howell with me.

Wouldn't you Know it – Glenn got a bite. It was a pretty good-sized bite at that. I told him not to reel it in until I got the camera out, and there I got maybe 90 seconds of film of Glenn catching a nice walleye – maybe a tad over seven pounds. A nice fish!

Well, that did it. No more fishing. Time to pack it in, drive back and get the film processed for the six p.m. news, which we did. We handed it to Adelson for his sports show, which that evening did Not include a golf tournament.

He ran it, and later told us he'd gotten a lot of Great compliments on it, and if we ever got any more to be sure that he got them and he'd run them.

OK – step back from this and contemplate what really happened here. Glenn and I decided to just chuck the news business and go fishing. So we did. On company time! In

204

filming him landing that fish, we documented our own screwing off for the afternoon.

But... it had Good Visual Values, and Adelson didn't have many fish films to use. So we were properly congratulated about that and told we'd done a great job.

Glenn and I have been chuckling about that ever since.

I got one in on my own one evening. I was the weatherman, and I believe Bob Kallberg was doing the news anchor. It was late July – the season of thunderstorms in North Dakota.

WDAY had, meanwhile, been quite proud of itself with its purchase of its first Weather Radar. Actually a USAF surplus radar from a bomber, nevertheless it had the only one in the valley. The station promoted it endlessly.

Came time for me to do the weather, and I noted that there was a line of thunderstorms moving southwest to northeast across the valley.

"There's one just north of Fargo that we here at Channel Four have been tracking for about an hour, using the latest in our weather-watching equipment. The window...."

I could hear Kallberg snort behind me, and the camera guy and control room types were hooting. Every now and then, you get in a good inside joke, even on-air.

We did do some good stuff. We drove out to central North Dakota and spent three days chasing down some rumors that there were some problems with the Garrison Diversion project. For those who weren't there, the Garrison Diversion wasn't so much a project as it was a religion in North Dakota. The upland dry farmers were going to get irrigation water from the Pick-Sloan dams along the Missouri, which would end the era of droughts (the dustbowl was still fresh in many people's minds) and this would then become the economic salvation of the state.

We were perhaps the first to suggest there might be a problem. Much to Schanzer's credit, he ran it as a five-part

205

series – two minutes or so a day – for a week. It caused Much consternation. U.S. Senator Milton Young called John Boler, who owned the station, to complain about it. Schanzer informed us we would probably not be doing a follow-up.

Eventually the problems with Garrison Diversion broke into wider circulation, and the project eventually stopped dead, with many of its canals and facilities never to be used.

Every now and again, we managed to do something right.

Briefly I was sent out to Bismarck to be the News Director for KXMB, Channel 12. Boler was selling it to Chet Reiten – a state senator out of Minot – and rather than send someone expensive to fill the slot, I was sent.

Back in Fargo, and the beginning of the end of my brief career in television. Boler, the station owner, had hired a News Consultant. These were miracle workers, at the time, who would critically evaluate and redesign the news bureaus of local television stations. Boler was tired of losing in the ratings to WDAY. He seemed not Quite to understand that Channel 4 was listed as being in Valley City (we rarely went near the place actually) rather than on Main Avenue in Fargo, so Fargoans were more used to watching Channel 6 than Channel 4.

He wanted higher ratings, which would mean More money.

The news consultant looked at our operation and concluded that we needed a prettier news anchor. So they hired a guy who really was a handsome fellow – but with perhaps the most obvious toupee around. He was, shall we say, somewhat less endowed with any actual Clue about Fargo-Moorhead, or the area, or the people, or the institutions in the area.

He was, in fact, the first actual Talking Head I'd ever met, and I took an instant dislike to him. He had trouble pronouncing words – we'd have to walk him through his news script before he could go on the air. His "happy talk" banter was stilted and forced. He made everyone else uncomfortable.

I told Boler I wanted a raise – to $10,000 a year. He fired me on the spot.

It was, as such things go, no great career loss. It was a silly job working for mostly silly people saying and doing mostly silly things.

Local television news was, at the time, little more than a local electronic headline service. There wasn't enough time actually to inform anyone about much of anything. But the time was filled, regardless.

Anyone who suspects they stayed Informed by watching local television news at the time deserves another think. They may have been amused or confused, but to my knowledge we seldom ever actually Informed anyone about much of anything. There was always less there than met the eye.

38.

Keeping Charlie Out of Casselton

***The Pentagon decreed the Fargo unit should
Blow Something Up.***

In the '60s and '70s, scrambling to get In to a Reserve or Guard unit was considered a preferable way of remaining out of actual danger, while still wearing a uniform.

So, if one wanted to maybe pick up six years of credit toward a federal retirement at age 65, plus make a few bucks every month by spending a weekend in a drill, the Reserve and Guard was the way to do it. In Fargo-Moorhead, there was an ongoing competition to get into the Reserve and Guard units, especially among the Good Families in town. It was difficult to be accepted – most applications for enlistment were routinely turned down, leaving the applicant eligible for the draft.

Those not having "connections" just didn't get in.

Just how it was at the time.

There were some amusing stories to come out of local Guard units – the best probably being the hapless pilot with the 119th fighter squadron out of Hector Airport. He had the misfortune of destroying five US aircraft in accidents during his flying career. That didn't make him a Bad Pilot – but it surely made him an Unlucky pilot. Something to be avoided. (If memory serves, he ran a local insurance agency in Fargo.)

The 119th retired him from flight status, and in the retirement celebration gave him a Certificate Suitable for Framing declaring him to be a Russian Fighter Ace. A singular achievement, but apparently the USAF didn't issue a ribbon for the accomplishment. A pity, really.

Returning veterans from Viet Nam at that stage of the war weren't terribly interested in re-enlisting in a local quasi-military unit all that much. I fell into that group – once I got back, I got rid of my uniforms (kept the boonie hat, which I still have) – just didn't much care to do that.

About five years later, the new Commanding Officer in the local Army Reserve unit wanted Non-Commissioned Officers with "combat experience" in the unit, perhaps to act as examples for those whose "military" experience involved drinking a lot of coffee and little else.

After being asked several times, I joined on a one-year trial basis, and started attending drills. To be honest, sitting around doing not much of anything on one weekend a month was boring. I didn't much care for the Wonderful Weekend Warrior mentality that seemed to affect the "leadership" of the unit. I was given my former rank – Sergeant E5 – and assigned to the Public Information Officer to write things. But there really was nothing to write about worth the effort.

With some other longer-term NCO's in the unit, we'd show up early Saturday morning for the roll call formation, get checked in, then stand around till about 10:00 or so, then leave for coffee and stay away most of the rest of the day, having lunch, visiting friends and generally not doing anything useful. For which I got a smallish paycheck once a month, and no one really said much of anything.

Only one really interesting memory came out of that year –
a good North Dakota story worth the telling:

The Army Reserve unit was classified as Combat Engineers.
The unit would practice building things, tearing things down,
digging holes with heavy equipment, filling holes with other
heavy equipment and everything else required to accomplish
those tasks and thereby ensure National Security. It was also
supposed to be able to Blow Something Up.

The Pentagon therefore decreed the Fargo unit should Blow
Something Up. Didn't much matter what – just so long as it
banged. But there were no local civic projects that could be
blown up, so the unit searched around to find Something,
Anything, that it could Blow Up for training purposes.

At the time, the rural areas within a 50-60 mile radius from
Fargo had a lot of old farmhouses, dating to the 1890s and early
1900s. Solid old things, made of true dimension lumber and
even forged square nails. Solid. Meant to last!

The unit found one somewhere southeast of Fargo, located
in a small draw sheltered from prairie winds. It had long since
been abandoned by its owners, and permission was sought and
obtained to Blow it Up. The regular Amy sent out a Master
Blaster to teach us how. This being an Actual Explosion, the
opportunity for great photos and even perhaps a film (we used
film cameras then) of the occasion was received with
considerable enthusiasm.

Came the Big Day and the unit moved some heavy
equipment in, to later bulldoze the scrap lumber left over into a
big pile. Everyone was deployed – even a field kitchen. We
were there fairly early in the morning, and spent several hours
just setting everything up.

The Master Blaster came with a bunch of explosives –
probably C4, but it could have been something else. All the
windows were knocked out of the building to reduce the

210

potential of flying glass. The interior was thoroughly inspected to ensure there was no remaining explosive or flammable materials inside that would increase Danger to the troops. The Master Blaster spent considerable time showing the unit's personnel the Precise placement of the charges, and the amount of material to be used to ensure that the structure blew up and then fell down properly. He gave quite the lecture on that. One must give him proper credit for safety – the Last thing a Reservist wanted was to be placed in Any danger at all, especially in a training accident.

It took a couple of hours to get everything properly emplaced. Horns and sirens were sounded, the unit was withdrawn to a safe distance, someone hollered "Fire in the hole!" and the detonator was pushed. Anticipation was great. There would soon be a fireball and lots of scrap wood flying through the air. We held our breaths....

There was a sort of muffled Boom, puffs of smoke came out of the windows, and three or four bricks fell off the chimney. That was it. Serious puzzlement followed.

An inspection of the structure showed little to no obvious structural damage. Some of the joints on the oak timbers used as floor joists and rafters had moved a little, but by and large the place was mostly intact. The Master Blaster concluded that Just Maybe he had underestimated the true strength of the building. Perhaps those square forged nails had a stronger hold in that old dry oak than he had figured.

So he reset the explosives, using considerably more this time, everyone withdrew a respectful distance, we had lunch (the guys called it Chow in a bow to genuine military language) and we reconnoitered to watch how This Time the event would come off Properly. Horns and sirens were sounded, someone yelled "Fire in the hole!" and the detonator was pushed.

211

Result: The chimney fell down completely. One wall bulged slightly. From a couple of hundred yards away, it was clear the old building was Not going to give up without a fight.

The Master Blaster was genuinely frustrated. It was, by then, getting on to about 2:00 in the afternoon, and, in order to get everyone back by quitting time (Reserve maneuvers ran according to a strict schedule as the troops had to get back to their families and jobs), the building had to be taken down ASAP.

This time, he held nothing back. He took All of his considerable remaining explosives stash, packed them carefully near the places where a beam had been knocked slightly loose and near places that showed at least Some evidence of damage from the previous two explosions. He made it clear that This Time the building Would go. Same procedure as before, and the detonator was pushed.

This time, the building surely Did blow up. As in maybe 300-400 feet in the air. Wood was flying all over hellandgone, and some pieces of it landed no more than Maybe 30-40 feet from the troops. Heavy equipment was brought in, the remains were dutifully shoved into a pile, and the unit left.

I really wanted The Story I was supposed to then write to be less about military prowess, and more about the wonderful strength of those old farmhouses that were Built To Last. The unit information officer did Not want to discuss how it took three tries to blow up an old farmhouse, so instead the story that went out was how this bunch of Combat Engineers spent a day blowing up an old farmhouse, how the effort was a Valuable Exercise in Military Proficiency, etc.

What Really happened is that an old North Dakota farmhouse withstood two attempts by modern explosives to blow it to smithereens, and it took three tries and four times as much explosives to finally take it apart.

There. I've finally gotten to write the truth.

I do believe the old settlers would have felt proud to know that.

I was mildly curious about the Army National Guard. There was a unit in Moorhead at the time – an Infantry unit that was a "roundout" to the 1st Infantry Division, aka the "Big Red One," I was familiar with from my time in Viet Nam. So I got out of the Reserve unit and signed up for the Guard.

First thing I noticed was that it had a Unit Flag with a bunch of campaign streamers on it. I looked some of them up. From the Civil War to World War II and perhaps beyond, several of them were related to rather well-known defeats and retreats and not the great victories that units prefer to celebrate. I didn't make a point of the campaign streamers in any of the releases I wrote for the unit.

I inquired into what were generously called Career Opportunities, and learned there were essentially none. I was expected to show up for the monthly drill, but not actually Do much of anything. I was assigned once again to the Public Information office, but did even less there than in the Reserve. So – show up Saturday morning bright and early, go through roll call, disappear for the rest of the day and show up again in the late afternoon or early evening for the evening formation, then repeat it all again on Sunday. I told the recruiter that I was interested in getting into some sort of Warrant Officer program, and was told that was reserved for others who had those slots wired for several years.

I went to Summer Camp at Camp Ripley over near Brainerd. Mostly uneventful, except for that duty I was given a squad of medics, a "Gamma Goat" – a sort of 6-wheel-drive ambulance – and a bunch of First Aid supplies and sent along with the mortar platoon to the range for firing exercises. The

213

idea was that in case someone got hurt, we'd take care of them and hustle them off to the hospital straightaway.

No one got hurt. Not even a bump or a bruise.

I met a guy from the Regular Army out of Ft. Riley, Kansas. A trained medic, but wanted to be a Real Soldier. His unit had operated out of Lai Khe, which I was in and out of often. He was all taken with someone who had been where his unit had previously been some few years earlier.

One of the traditions of summer camp was that at some point, some force would ambush one of the units on patrol, and pretend to kill them in a properly loud and obnoxious military manner. But the CO decreed that This year, there would be no such ambush, so people could relax. My experience was that soldiers in the field should Never relax. So my buddy and I got a tad faced one evening, and decided that if no one else would do a proper ambush, the two of us would.

We got some artillery simulators – a sort of large firecracker that would make a sound like an incoming artillery shell then give off a loud Bang and flash – and some other pretend ordinance, got into our web gear, painted our faces black, loaded a couple of rifles with blanks, and the two of us ambushed a sleeping unit all camped out in the woods. Even the guards were sleeping!

We set off fireworks, fired our blank-filled rifles into the air, shouted a bunch of stuff and ran around raising hell. After no more than 5-6 minutes, we got the hell Out of there, got back to our units, cleaned our faces, put away our equipment and sat around listening to the resulting noise.

Next morning, some Lieutenant Colonel read the unit out, and wanted to know Just Who Did This!

We never said a word about it, and the matter was left unresolved. No one ever did figure out who did it.

214

My real function soon became clear. I was a decoration. Being one of the few NCO's with actual combat experience, more than once I was told to report to the unit CO in my Class A dress uniform – the one with the ribbons on it. So when/if some visiting elected official showed up, I was to attend and stand around, be introduced as a War Hero and that would make the CO look good.

I hated doing that! It seemed demeaning, somehow. Still does.

The same CO ordered a One-Mile Run. This was a cause for some concern amongst the troops. First off, it was Hot that week. Second, a good many of the troops were somewhat past the bloom of Youth, and were to be frank mostly out of condition or downright lard-assed. No way they could run a mile.

At Camp Ripley, there were some quadrangles in the cantonment area that were right at a quarter mile on a side. One trip around was one mile. The allowable time for the "run" was to be 15 minutes – equivalent to four miles/hr. Not much more than a brisk walk. I knew from having been on the ROTC Drill Team while back in college that if they would just march at a little bit better than a normal pace, they could get around the mile in just about the allotted time. I got about 25-30 of them together and told them that when they came to the run, they should find me and I'd ensure they came through OK.

At the run, the front was full of Young Men who were In Shape, and various people bragged who would be first to complete the run. In combat boots, trousers left open at the bottom and T-shirts, five minutes would get a bunch of them to the finish line. That wasn't even a distant hope for my lard-assed platoon.

The starting gun fired, and the younger guys took off at a fast pace in 85+ degree temperatures. I got my contingent into a

215

5 x 6 column, and started them marching in a regular constant pace. I called cadence – the Hut Two Three Four thing – and we even did some singing.

We were dead last in the run from the start, and we stayed that way. I kept track on my stopwatch about our progress, and we were doing just fine. I had it figured pretty much to the second.

A little before the halfway mark, along came a jeep with a couple of officers in it, and one of them asked (in a loud military manner) "What's going on here, sergeant? This is a run, and these men are supposed to be running!" I responded that they had fifteen minutes allotted to get to the finish line, assured the officer that they would be there on time, gave him a snappy salute, and caught up with my group.

We kept marching, at a measured pace. Along the route, we found several people who had stopped to puke, and invited them into our group. So we had perhaps 35-40 people as we approached the finish.

I noticed, as we approached the finish line, that we were perhaps twenty seconds ahead of the allowed time, so just yards before the finish, I gave them a "To the rear, march!" command, marched them in that for 7-8 seconds, then gave it again. The last guy in the group crossed the finish line about 3-4 seconds before the finishing gun fired. The guys in the group came around to thank me for keeping them from having heart attacks. None were even out of breath.

There was this Major who found me, stood me to Attention and asked just Whathehell I was doing right there at the end of the event. I told him I ensured the guys that they would make it within the elapsed time, and they all did. Did the Major perhaps feel that the timing was wrong?

"I supposed you figure that little march to the rear was funny," he said in his most severe accusatory tone.

"Well, yes sir – I did. And still do. They all made it within the allotted time, and that was all that was required."

He was Not at all happy, but there wasn't One Damned Thing he could do about it, so I was summarily dismissed and he walked resolutely away. I was told later that the unit CO was not at All pleased with how it all worked out. I didn't really care. My Guys made it!

In the end, I left the Guard unit too. Over the next several years, a bunch who had joined the Reserve or Guard to avoid being sent to Viet Nam had their enlistments run out, and they too just got along with their lives. Having served while Viet Nam was going on, naturally their kids asked questions of them later. I recall one guy telling me of one exchange with his daughter.

"Daddy – what did you do in the Viet Nam war?" she asked.

"I kept Charlie out of Casselton."

Mission accomplished.

39.

I Demand a Recount

It had Never once occurred to me I might actually win.

It happened by accident. Honest.

Fargoans Love their politics. Local, state or federal – Fargo (and Cass County, once known as Imperial Cass in the legislature because the delegation was ten per cent of the entire state legislature) were the state's local version of the Great Eastern Liberal Conspiracy. For decades, Fargo managed to carve itself something called a "multi-senatorial district" for legislators. That meant that in all the rest of North Dakota, state senators had to run in individual districts, but in Fargo, all five ran together – a sort of small "at large" district, the purpose of which was to ensure that to the maximum degree possible, the entire slate of five senators could be controlled by one political party.

That would be the Republicans.

Over time, the local Rs began to see this status as a sort of special right, exclusive to Fargo legislators. Attempts to change it in the legislature got blocked. There were several court challenges to it, but by and large those never really were taken seriously. The multi-senate district remained – five senators and ten state representatives, controlled for decades by one party.

It was 1974. Richard Nixon had just resigned in disgrace, and most people across the nation were pretty much disgusted with Republicans. I was then 30 years old – and was similarly affected. I was personally Outraged that the Rs in the White House had attempted to undermine the fundamental political process that undergirds the entire idea of representative democracy in the country, and I really and truly mostly just wanted to yell at somebody. I'd never been openly partisan before, and had always considered myself more a Moderate Extremist, philosophically, than anything else.

I was then a graduate student, married only a couple of years, no party ties, had no money, no connections and was hardly a prime political candidate for any office. I lived in an apartment in West Fargo, and had no community ties there to speak of, either.

The Fargo Democrats, happily, provided just about the perfect venue for being able to yell at the Rs for a while, without having to deal with anything as important as raising substantial money toward a campaign that wasn't going to win anyway. It was about as safe a prospect as there could be. Get endorsed by the local D convention, file for the office, make some appearances and speeches here and there, lose and get on with my life.

What could be better than that?

I told several of my friends at NDSU what I was planning to do, but that I didn't figure it would interfere with the classes I was taking. It was going to be more of a spare-time project than anything serious. "You're nuts!" was the reply. "What if you win?"

219

The question simply had never occurred to me. In that district the Republicans always won. They always would. The answer was obvious.

I got to the Democratic convention that evening – it was in the basement of the Civic Auditorium if memory serves. A friend was ready to put my name into nomination for a state representative endorsement. But the Ds were having trouble finding five people to nominate for the senate positions, so I told my friend to go ahead and nominate me for that one – which would then leave a representative position open for someone else.

That's how I became a candidate for the North Dakota State Senate. In reality, I figured, losing in the general election would be not much different from losing a state representative seat, so what the hell – six of one and all. Let the campaign commence!

That's when things began to go all wrong.

Bill Guy, a former Democratic governor of North Dakota, was going to run for the U.S. Senate, and was going to pull a Lot of money into the state. Much of it, quite wisely, was going to go to a large Get Out The Vote campaign in his behalf, and the chances were pretty good that legislative candidates were going to get a boost out of that down ballot too. We did.

I raised a modest amount (the largest contribution was $150) of money, and took out as my sole advertising a half page in the Midweek Eagle – the local advertising paper distributed free to Fargo and West Fargo. For a small sum, I could control my own copy and say whatever I wanted. Besides, Wayne Lubenow – formerly a writer for The Forum – had his own weekly column in it. Between that and the classified ads, it was reasonably well read pretty much across the city.

But as for regular newspapers or direct mail or even radio – no, that was Way too expensive to consider. Television would have been unthinkable.

(I had been gone from KXJB for more than a year by the time the campaign was underway, but I suspect that former job did give me a leg up on name recognition – which is an important thing all on its own.)

My weekly Midweek column apparently really bothered some of the local Rs. I didn't care. I wrote it, all on my own, asked no one else's permission to say what I wanted to say the way I wanted to say it. It was all mine. This was what I'd had in mind all along.

I clearly recall one occasion, though – a Candidate's Luncheon sponsored by the local Chamber of Commerce. Now everyone was fully aware that the CoC was in lockstep with the local Rs, but in the Spirit of Fair Play they invited both the Ds and Rs to attend and say a few words. My recollection is both clear and correct in this – they treated the Ds with considerable disrespect at that meeting, and me with near contempt. One of the R candidates essentially made fun of "this young man" who really had no experience and didn't know much, having the Gall to be discussing some of the issues facing the state from a viewpoint of something other than good sound Republican orthodoxy.

Well, what the hell anyway. I knew I'd signed up for some of this, and on all of those occasions, I gave as good as I got when it came to discussing the specific issues. At the time, much of that was about coal gasification, but there were also discussions involving education, state spending generally (and the general previous Cass delegation opposition to funding the State Fair in Minot – the cause of some general resentment toward Imperial Cass from across the rest of the state.)

There was one more thing. I knocked on six thousand doors across Fargo and West Fargo, and personally asked people to vote for me. The Fargo Republican candidates were Much too important to do the same on that scale. That may have mattered.

Came election night, and the Ds were having a Victory Party over at the Town House motel in Fargo. I attended, of course – I sort of had to. I had put together a couple of short comments discussing my own personal reaction to losing, prepared to congratulate the Republican candidates on winning yet again and like that.

My brother, Larry, was that evening a roving live reporter for KFGO radio, and as luck would have it he was assigned to be the reporter at the Town House. He had a better line to the county election office than pretty much anyone else, via his 2-way radio hookup, and he got the returns faster than the folks writing on the boards at the D's party.

There came a point in the evening when I heard him calling my name, so I stopped to talk with him and was mildly surprised when he stuck a microphone in my face and started an actual interview.

"Well, Mr. Homuth – it looks like All five of the Democratic State Senate candidates have been elected. This is a stunning upset. What do you plan to do now that you're a State Senator?"

What did I plan? I didn't Plan anything! This was, to be quite honest about it, unthinkable. I knew that, because I'd never once even thought about it. But there I was, with a Live microphone stuck in my face, and I knew I had to say something. But what?

So I said – live on the radio – the first thing that came to my mind:

"I'm going to demand a recount."

Yes – those were the first words out of my mouth as a Senator elect. I don't know that I was fully conscious when I spoke them, so surprised I was If this were true. There was a piece of me that thought he was just pulling my leg – faking an interview as a sort of fraternal prank. He shut the mike off.

"That just went out Live on the air," he said, laughing about it. He thought that I was deliberately trying to be funny. I wasn't. I wasn't quite certain at that very moment that this was the outcome I wanted at all. I knew, from having reported on the 1971 and 1973 legislative sessions, what was involved in Being A Legislator, and something about what it was going to cost me.

But damn it all – I had won. That just Has to be good, right? Just about that time, the news got to the rest of the party, and it erupted in loud cheering, and Larry and I lost track of each other for the rest of the evening. There was much back-patting and congratulating and hand-shaking going on and people calling me Senator Homuth.

That took some getting used to, I can tell you.

Of the immediate aftermath, memories are a little crowded. Of the five Democrats running for the State Senate, I got the lowest overall vote total. But it was more than any of the five Republicans running, so I was duly elected.

It did get quite satisfactorily better between then and the beginning of the legislative session, however. The Chamber of Commerce put together another luncheon – this time to deal with the newly elected legislators, and not just mere candidates.

I recall being struck by how, in only a few short weeks, I was considered Far more knowledgeable, and Far more informed, and Far more mature and fundamentally Far more important than I was as a candidate. The treatment was nearly effusive, it was so mannerly and proper. What a change, in so short a time!

One of my newly-elected colleagues was overwhelmed by the honor. "I can hardly believe we're Senators!" she said. I took some pains to give her a smallish reality test. "We are who we have always been," I said. "Just temporarily, we have been given permission to play in a public sandbox that few others

223

ever get to see. Don't get too carried away with the honor. It's a lot of work."

History does not, I suspect, record many instances where the winner of an election's first public comment on being told he had won said he might want to demand a recount. At the time, many who knew me thought it was just Homuthian Humor. But I can tell you in all candor, it had Never once occurred to me that I might actually win.

I was due to join the legislative session in Bismarck in early January. I had to rent a place to live, had to re-do my own personal schedule, withdraw from my graduate classes (I never went back to them later on), discuss how to handle this with my wife – just a whole raft of things I never figured I'd have to deal with. It was nearly overwhelming.

What made it fully overwhelming was worse. I had now come to the attention of Powers That Be across the state, and was getting a lot of mail, a lot of phone calls, invitations to this and that event, requests for private conferences and meetings all over the place and suddenly my previously unstressed world became a most complicated place indeed.

In the organizational session in December, we all went out to get a tour of the capitol, apply for and get our committee assignments, pick the place where we would sit, sign up for the stationery and notepads, get an idea of how things were done and pose for the official pictures.

I asked for and got the two committees I wanted – the Major committee was Industry, Business and Labor and the Minor committee was Agriculture. My sense was that these two committees would be closer to the economy and lives of most North Dakotans than any others. Much to my surprise, the Republicans – who may have lost Fargo, but still controlled the state – put me on both of them.

I surprised a number of people by choosing Not to sit with the rest of the Democrats in the Senate chamber. There were only 17 of us, and 34 Republicans. The Ds sort of clustered together in a tight knot just to the left of the middle aisle in the Senate Chamber. I chose instead a seat far over to the right, just in front of Pete Naaden, one of The most conservative Rs in the place. I had two good reasons for doing this: First, I didn't really care to hang out with S.F. Hoffner, the D minority leader. He was just a bit too smooth for me. Second, I figured that clustering like that would lead to too much group-think and attempts to control us as a block of votes. But there wasn't enough of that block to be bothered about.

We didn't have our own offices. We didn't have legislative aides to do the staff work. If we wanted to correspond, we had to write something up, and one of the secretaries in the pool would type it for us. Which meant that anything we wrote back to a constituent would be known by the Republicans immediately – they hired all the personnel. (Remember – I was no mere neophyte in all of this. Having been a news reporter in the previous two sessions gave me an insight into how the place Really worked that few others had.)

The only appropriate punishment for someone who runs for public office is to have them win it. I was about to receive mine.

40.

Fargo State Senator

The sort of 'insider baseball' that gets discussed in legislatures, mostly out of sight and comprehension of news reporters and the voters generally... a swing of tens of millions hanging on it...

Just prior to the start of the legislative session in January, the legislative affairs director for the Fargo Chamber of Commerce met with me to discuss a list of ten legislative priorities for the chamber. I read the list, considered it carefully before our meeting, and at the meeting made my stance quite plain.

I would support four of the initiatives out of hand, oppose three no matter what, and I was prepared to hear more information on the other three, and would make my decision after that had been done. He told me that was perhaps the most straightforward reply he had ever received, and thanked me for being so direct. (In the fullness of time, I did go with the three I was uncertain about, but only after they had been carefully amended in the committee process. There was no payoff for that. I never got a dime or a vote from anyone in the chamber. I keep my promises, even to my opponents. I considered it a matter of honor. Mine. I did Not wish to become a real e.e. cummings' politician.)

Early on in the session, one of the bills I said I would support was to free state banks in North Dakota from the arbitrary limit on interest they could charge on loans. Previously the Ds had opposed raising that limit, but the argument made No sense at all. The idea was to allow the state-chartered banks to float their interest rates charged and paid according to Federal Reserve Regulation Q. Other than a few minor tweaks, it was the first bill the Industry, Business and Labor (IBL) Committee passed out with a Do Pass recommendation.

The chair – quite a capable fellow, Emil Kautzmann of Mandan – asked for volunteers to carry the bill on the floor. I was one of those to raise my hand. He was, to be honest, somewhat surprised at that. I was a freshman, far and away the youngest in the Senate, and to him an unknown quantity. It was tradition in the Senate to harass a freshman senator bringing a bill to the floor with endless questions, and even an initial vote defeating the bill. Just one of those Good Ol' Boy traditions. I knew about it, having seen it happen in the two previous sessions.

I was, however, a Democrat, and that did matter. Governor Art Link was also a Democrat, and there was always the chance that if the bill came out of the legislature without bipartisan support for it, he would veto it. The veto might well have held. Not many at the time really understood that artificially limiting the competitiveness of state-chartered banks could hurt their customers, who would respond by moving their money to federally-chartered banks instead.

(Isn't this Great stuff? This is the sort of 'insider baseball' that gets discussed in legislatures, mostly out of sight and comprehension of news reporters and the voters generally.

Nevertheless, there is a swing of tens of millions hanging on it, and that decidedly does matter.)

The IBL Chair said he would allow me to carry the bill on the floor, and that should there be any problem, he was fully prepared to backstop me on anything technical that might come up. The lobbyist for the ND Bankers Association was somewhat fretful – he wasn't sure about this either, but the lure of bipartisan support for perhaps The most important legislation they were after was so strong that he, too, said if I needed any further information, he'd be happy to provide it.

I didn't know what all the fuss was about. The bill was quite clear – refreshingly so, in fact. Its purpose was specific, its impact known. It wasn't really rocket science. It was just really important.

So the time came, early in the session, and I stood up to explain the bill on the Senate floor. I had prepared exhaustively for the effort. I had pared down the presentation to several specific points, followed all the appropriate speechifying protocols, and asked for questions.

Essentially, there were none. There wasn't even much of an attempt to undertake the traditional hazing on the matter. One Senator asked me something about some other Federal Reserve regulation, and whether or not it applied. But it was clear that his point was simply non-germane to the bill at hand, and that was my answer.

The bill passed. With good bipartisan support.

I got a note from the committee chair thanking me for an excellent presentation, and another from the Bankers Association lobbyist commending me for my good work. Later on, during a recess, a couple of members and reporters repeated essentially the same thing, all of them expressing considerable surprise that I had done this rather competently.

I don't know what they were expecting – it's not as though it was difficult. It just needed to be done well, and I remain pleased to this day that I was able to rise to the occasion. For that ability, I have since thanked the Excellent education I got in the Fargo Public School System, and the instruction I got at NDSU especially from the speech teacher, E. James Ubbelohde, who more than anyone else taught me how to be erudite – to speak clearly and plainly, and whenever possible, briefly, on pretty much any matter. I've never believed that I alone could take credit for whatever those skills have allowed me to accomplish.

One more bit of "insider baseball" worth the telling:

There were quite literally dozens of bills having to do with strip mining, coal gasification and related matters during the session. Most of those went to committees other than the ones I was on. But one came through and somehow ended up on the Senate Agriculture Committee – chaired by Ken Morgan.

No offense to Ken, but he was prepared to talk about Farming, not Mining or anything related to it. So he was uncertain of what to do, as were the other Rs on the committee, who were also mostly farmers.

He asked if I could handle the hearing. He couldn't appoint me as a subcommittee chair – I was of the Wrong Party for him to do that. But he could appoint another R to chair the subcommittee, who could then excuse himself from the hearing and leave the gavel with me. So I ended up "chairing" a subcommittee, without actually being appointed to do so.

The bill came at the request of the State Geologist office. Fundamentally they wanted to get the information about coal deposits that the mining companies had. They saw no sense in trying to replicate the exploration efforts on their own, and they didn't have either the funding or the time to do it, anyway. They wanted to know what the mining companies knew.

The coal mining companies were having none of that. They feared, quite reasonably, that if the information got into a state agency, it would thereafter be made public. Since it had been gotten at their own cost and effort across years, they considered it proprietary – and surely that was correct.

On the other hand, the People of North Dakota relied on the State Geologist to be capable of reasonable regulation of mining efforts, or if not that, at least Knowing before the fact what sort of impacts could be expected as the mining expanded.

That was the issue. The matter seemed intractable.

Came the time for the subcommittee to meet, and I ended up with the gavel. The table was T-shaped – the state agency types arrayed down the right hand side and the coal company lobbyists (they wore Great suits!) down the left.

I opened up the proceedings with these words:

"We have before us Senate Bill (something or other) for consideration. Make no mistake, when this committee rises (yeah – that's how we talked) there Will be a bill to recommend to the full Senate. In broad terms, it will require the coal companies make available to the State Geologist current and future information on coal deposits in the state. The State Geologist will be required to hold all such information confidential and proprietary. The term of the bill will be for ten years, with allowable extensions year by year for the following five, at which point after fifteen years the information will pass into the public domain.

"We may discuss at length the details on precisely How to do that, and this subcommittee is prepared to take as much time as necessary today, this afternoon, this evening and working into tomorrow to get there. But we Will accomplish this task. Is that clear to everyone?"

I suspect they were mildly shocked at the tone, but it did nicely focus everyone's attention on the task at hand. So we all got to work, and in only three or so hours, we had a bill draft that seemed acceptable to all around the table. I adjourned the meeting, and prepared to go to lunch prior to the afternoon floor session.

The lobbyists all expressed their surprise that things had gone as well as they did. The State Geologist rep said he was pleased that it hadn't become a completely contentious matter.

The bill went before the full agriculture committee and passed without a dissenting vote. It was then due to go before the full Senate for final passage. Everything seemed to be going well.

The very next morning, the lobbyist for North American Coal ambushed me in the corridor. "Senator Homuth," he said, "I've been in touch with the corporate headquarters, and they said they still find the bill objectionable and can't support it."

I pondered that for a bit. I had walked the bill through the D caucus, and gotten full support for it. Ken had recommended it likewise to the Rs as well. Our count said we had the votes to pass it as it was, without further amendment. We were Not about to pull it back into committee just to satisfy the whim of a single coal company, no matter what size it was.

I asked him whom he had discussed this with. He said something like the Vice President of something or other. I then did something mildly out of character for me, but it seemed useful at the time:

"Well, give him this message for me – exactly as I'm giving it to you. Tell him to go (insert the f-bomb here) himself. I've got the votes, and the bill Will pass as is."

(Fact of the matter was, I was offended at this corporate type trying to jack me around, and was having none of it. I don't often get angry, but was prepared to make an exception in this instance.)

231

"You tell him that – Exactly as I said it. That bill is going to pass. Period."

Later on that afternoon, he caught me again in the corridor between the two chambers. "I gave him your message, exactly as you said it."

"And what was his response?" I asked.

"He said, 'Well, I guess the little bastard has got us by the short hairs. Let it go'."

We shook hands, and got on with the day's business. I don't recall what happened to the bill over on the House side, but I don't recall any major changes. All in all, not a bad outcome.

There are many such "insider baseball" stories that could be told about the legislative process. Too many to discuss here, and to be honest there were so many I don't recall all of them clearly. Those two stand out, though.

As I mentioned, we had no secretaries to handle correspondence, so while sitting in my rented house in the evenings, I would read my mail and hand-write responses on my official stationery. Mostly I printed, and mostly short responses. If someone asked me to support something I supported, I said I would. If they wanted me to support something I didn't support, I said I wouldn't.

One letter, though, stands out in my memory as exceptional, even now.

The big fiscal discussion in the 1975 session was on aid to school districts. Fargo had an "unlimited mill levy" – it could fund its schools at whatever level the voters might choose to support. That provision predated statehood, and was grandfathered into the state constitution.

Other rural districts, however, had to request permission to increase the local mill levy – read Property Tax – for school support. The state legislature considered simply appropriating money to local schools to offset rising costs – something I considered then (and now) a most reasonable proposal.

I got this letter from a guy in Fargo. It said essentially that Much of the money spent on education is wasted, and there was no teacher in the entire state worth more than ten thousand dollars a year, and he Demanded (no less) that I oppose any such "equalization" money for schools across the state.

I don't recall exactly – I might have felt offended at that, or perhaps I was in a bad mood, or maybe I was just amused by so fully ignorant a statement. So I hand-wrote a reply that went something like this:

"Dear ….. – I agree – much of the money spent on education is clearly wasted. Take, for example, the money spent on Your education….." I ended up by saying something about how it was my intent to vote for school equalization funds. I figured that settled that, and I'd hear no more about it. (Truth was, we all got a lot of such letters and they mostly went unanswered straight into the Crackpot File. I don't recall why I answered his.)

It was maybe two weekends later, during one of those district town hall meetings in Fargo. No matter – it's what happened next that was the most fun.

We did our little spiels and the floor was opened to local folks to ask questions, make statements or whatever. Eventually this guy got up to speak – and wouldn't you know it was the same guy to whom I'd sent the letter.

"I want you all to know what sort of an a**hole Senator Homuth really is!"

Good start! I knew what was coming, and cringed. This was Not going to go well at all.

And he read the letter verbatim, and held it up for all to see.

I cringed even more. Then the Fates stepped in and rescued the entire situation, much to my considerable surprise.

It turned out that at this particular meeting, the Fargo teachers had decided to show up en masse, and they thought my answer to the guy was...well...fully supportable and great fun. The place erupted in Howls of laughter, and the guy got all red-faced, muttered something unintelligible and stomped out of the place in a state if high dudgeon.

I got a lot of kudos for that from the teachers, and even the Forum reporter said he thought it was really funny, but had no intention of writing it up. Which was just fine with me.

I was not cut out for any sort of political career. I became a politician mostly by accident, was a reasonably competent legislator, but to be frank, I had just No patience with many of The Voters whose complete lack of information and coherence was something that, to be honest, I found offensive.

There are those who hold elected office who can suffer fools gladly.

I've never been able to suffer them at all.

It's not that I lack manners. Mom taught me how useful those are early on, and whenever faced with a situation where they're called for, I can be downright courtly. I'm not mean-spirited – I wish no one any harm from my actions, and go rather out of my way to avoid it whenever possible. But egregious stupidity, regardless of its sources, is just something that ought not to be pandered to, as I see it.

I loved Being a legislator. I knew how to do it, knew the consequences of my actions, and found the outcomes most satisfying. It was the campaigning I didn't care for. I didn't like sucking up to anyone while begging for contributions (really Investments, from the donor's frame of reference) so I could continue in office another term. I didn't like trying to keep a straight face while listening to some poor clueless twit utter a blast of inchoate nonsense unrelated to the matter at hand.

But while holding the office, I considered it my Duty to those who put their trust in me to represent them as well as I could, and I came out of that session with the sense that I had held true to that personal commitment as best I could.

The session eventually ended. I went home, but couldn't turn off the emotional high. So I went skiing for a week, just to burn it off. It helped. I had two more years left of a four-year term, though. I dreaded the interim till the next session.

41.

One of the Two Best Things

*"The only problem with Doing Good is that people
expect you to do it more than once."*

Dave Bateman, a radio personality back in Fargo well into the
'70s once told me that over lunch. He was a fascinating guy –
born in Oil Trough, Arkansas, spoke with a pronounced drawl,
active in the local Shriners in Fargo and wandered around in a
large Stetson or Resistol hat whenever he was in public.

I was privileged to Do Good on a large-scale twice – once in
the legislature, and once again shortly after leaving. This is the
story of the first.

Senate Bill 2222 in the 1975 session required insurance
companies offering health insurance to offer coverage for mental
health, drug addiction and alcoholism. Just that simple –
nothing else. It didn't set any dollar limits on the coverage – just
required that it be offered.

It came to the Senate Industry, Business and Labor
Committee fairly early in the session that year, and was
supported by the North Dakota Mental Health Association
(NDMHA). Their lobbyist, Myrt Armstrong, gave a quite
passionate testimony supporting the bill in front of the

committee, as did several other medical providers who suggested that the need for these three things were rapidly increasing in North Dakota.

Testifying in opposition were, naturally, the health insurance companies. They just didn't want to do it, and said so directly.

The IBL committee pondered that at length, and after considerable deliberation weighing the potential outcomes for ordinary folks against the objections of the insurance industry, passed the bill on to the full Senate with a "Do Pass" recommendation. It passed the full Senate by a healthy margin – I have a vague memory that the vote in favor was unanimous – and the bill was sent over to the House side for further consideration. That's where it ran into trouble.

One way to kill a bill is just to vote it down as it is. The other way is to deliberately enlarge it, make it Complex and Wonderful, stuff it with more provisions than were ever intended, then present the bloated bill and have it voted down because it was far too over-reaching.

When SB2222 got to the House, instead of being sent to the House IBL Committee, where it normally would have gone as being a simple business regulation, it was instead sent to the Social Welfare Committee. The members of that committee proceeded straightaway to including a longish list of other provisions and demands on the insurance industry. I suspect the members did so simply because they were not seeing the bill as a simple business regulation, but rather as some sort of larger social policy agenda item.

The House killed it.

When that vote was taken, I ran into Myrt in the corridor, and she was in tears. This had been The main legislative goal of the NDMHA, and she believed it had been entirely lost for that session. She was nearly beside herself at the loss.

I told her not to worry – there was a Plan B. She asked what it was. I told her just to sit tight and watch. Things had to happen in a bit of a hurry, since it was getting close to the end of the session.

The House IBL committee had earlier sent over its own bill on a related, though somewhat less comprehensive, matter. It had passed the full House, and was sitting in the Senate IBL committee without further action. If memory serves – and it may well not – that bill was House Bill 1546. (The session laws of 1975 would probably give the correct bill number, but for this writing, it's HB 1546.)

This is where a pretty good knowledge of legislative procedure makes it possible to do some useful work.

I got together with the Chair of the Senate IBL committee, and reminded him that we had passed SB 2222 out of committee and it had passed the full Senate overwhelmingly. I told him what had happened to it in the House, and focused on the way the SB went to a different committee entirely. But now we had HB 1546 in hand, and the Senate IBL committee could still amend it, and if the Senate passed the bill as amended, it would then return to the House, where it would go to the House IBL Committee, and not the Social Welfare Committee.

Still with me?

So the Senate IBL Committee did what is known as a "gut and stuff." We passed an amendment to HB 1546 that read in part "Delete everything after the words A Bill, and insert in lieu thereof….." and we inserted the full text of SB 2222 as it had originally passed the Senate. So SB 2222 was still alive, but now it had a HB number and would return to the House IBL Committee as amended. The Senate passed it – again.

A little work with the Chair of the House IBL Committee ended up by approving the Senate Amendments, and the motion

238

to the floor was to concur with the Senate amendments to HB 1546 and pass it as amended.

The amendments were concurred with and the bill passed the House as amended. Having now passed both the Senate and the House with identical language, the bill was duly engrossed and sent to the Governor for his signature, which it got.

Mind you – this all happened fairly quickly. I had alerted Myrt to watch for it and to get her supporters in line, but not to make too much fuss for fear of attracting too much attention, She couldn't quite believe that it would work. But it did. The next time I saw her, she had tears as well, but for an entirely different and better reason than before.

If I may be slightly snarky for just a bit, one of the most gratifying personal outcomes of all of that was when Rep. "Aloha" Eagles heard about it. Her husband was the head of the Blue Cross in North Dakota, and part of her actions were to ensure that nothing got passed in the legislature that the company didn't support.

She just never saw it coming. She was, according to friends, still acting Most pleased about having SB 2222 killed, when someone told her that it had actually passed, only under a different bill number.

She caught me in the corridor and read me out pretty severely for a "sneaky trick" in getting the bill passed. I just smiled, and said "Better luck next time."

So folks with health insurance got coverage for mental health, drug addiction and alcoholism after that. All in all, not a bad day's work.

A popular quote, ofttimes misattributed to Otto von Bismarck, reads "Those who love the law, and sausage, should never see either being made." Precisely so – the process can be unattractive. But the key matter is the quality of the sausage – and, as in this case, the law.

42.

You Can Win for Losing

I think I did the right thing. Reluctantly, I will admit.

Not long after I became a State Senator, the Republicans, who had theretofore defended the multi-senatorial district in Fargo, changed their minds. The fact that it was clear they could lose all five seats simultaneously may have had something to do with that. But in a court case, the local Rs switched sides, and lo and behold, the multi-senate district was struck down and five districts were formed from the old one. I had to run again to finish my 4-year term.

My wife and I had, meanwhile, decided to buy a house, and we'd found a smallish place on 12th Avenue North, right across the street from NDSU's Minard Hall parking lot. (That house is gone now – the university bought it and some adjacent houses and built a strip mall.) Our new residence put me into the district that included NDSU, and there was no other incumbent senator in it.

That wasn't the reason we bought it. We bought it because (a) it was inexpensive – something like $20,000 or so, roomy enough, had a two-car garage and a nice-sized lot, and (b) we could get it on a contract for deed. At the time, getting conventional financing was a mountain we were not prepared to climb. My wife was then in Law School at UND, and money wasn't exactly plentiful.

I was then working on a grant-funded project for NDSU, so I was a member of the staff, but not the faculty. It also made for a nice short walk to work – five minutes tops.

I kept attending the legislative interim study committee meetings all through the rest of 1975 and early 1976. I also had to do the "creamed chicken" circuit because I had become a Person Of Consequence. There were more such meetings and invitations than I ever cared to attend, but it was an obligation and duty, and not a mere choice. So I went.

In retrospect, I suspect that was pretty stupid of me, though no more stupid than running for the office in the first place. I placed a higher priority on that than attending to my marriage. I wish I hadn't done that now. I didn't know better at the time.

As the election campaign season drew close in 1976, one of my other earlier colleagues, Rod Schuster, decided not to run for re-election. He was still setting up his law practice, and had other things to attend to. Smart man, with a good set of priorities.

I was torn. Part of me so very much enjoyed Being A Senator that I wouldn't have minded at all doing it again. But there was that other part – the realist – that recognized that really I was a fish out of water, Being A Politician wasn't really my forte' and that I should simply not run for reelection.

A day or so prior to the endorsing convention, I called together the chair of the district Democratic Party along with a couple of others, and told them that I had pretty much decided not to run again – that I had some other things to do in my life that I should be getting on with.

They disagreed. For several hours, they regaled me with how very much they respected my work, yadda yadda yadda.

In essence, I could very nearly walk on water, I was a great carrier of the Democratic Tradition, my presence would be missed, and so on and so on.

I now regret to say it, but they talked me back into running again. I wish now I'd simply stood by my guns, recognized my own limitations and not done it. Once in it, Politics can be pretty heady stuff for the psychologically unprepared. At 32, I was psychologically unprepared for that kind of effusive praise. It was probably quite sincere – they all meant well. I doubt there was a duplicitous thought in their heads. Such is the credibility we place on those whom we elect to represent us.

It just wasn't wise.

Two bad things happened during the campaign.

First, the grant I was working under ran out as of July, and I was unemployed for a period. I applied for and took unemployment to tide me over for a while. I had bills to pay, little to no savings to fall back on and needed the money. A reporter for the Fargo Forum, Kevin Carvell – my predecessor as editor of the NDSU Spectrum, you may recall, the guy who started Zip to Zap – apparently got the story from someone who leaked it to him, and it hit the front page. I was embarrassed at having this part of my personal life made public, especially when the chair of the local Republicans made several snarky comments about it. I eventually, before the election, landed another job I had earlier applied for, but the damage was done. It wasn't fatal, but it was dispiriting.

I also had pneumonia for three weeks. That meant I couldn't knock on doors, attend campaign events or do anything else other than sit at home wishing I were anywhere else but there. However, since I was aware that Death is Nature's Way of telling you to slow down, and fully recognizing that the immediate cause of my Dad's death was pneumonia, I stayed put and recovered as best I could.

I lost. By 19 votes across the district. Close, but no cigar. I had carried the city portion of the district quite handily, but lost the campus vote. A little strange, but not outside the realm of possibility.

Well, that was OK at the time. I was asked if I was going to request a recount this time – which I thought was mildly humorous, given my earlier response to winning. Frankly, I was relieved more than I thought I might be. I said No – I'll just let it stand, and was fully prepared to let it go at that.

Which is how things stayed for a while. Then I started to pick up on the rumors of How the election on the campus had gone, and that piqued my curiosity.

At the time, NDSU published a Student Handbook (generally called the Stud Book, doubtless a reference to the animal husbandry practiced by a good many students of the university, which not that much earlier had been known as the Agricultural College). It contained the names and home towns of every student on the campus.

North Dakota did not, and still does not, I am told, have voter registration. You could just show up at the polls, give them an ID of a local residence and vote. The names of each person voting were kept in a Precinct Book, which was public information and available to anyone who wanted to examine it. On catching wind of these rumors, I surely did.

I took a fresh copy of the Stud Book and carefully put a dot with a green marker by every student who voted on the campus in that election. There were, if memory serves, just something short of 300 or so who had.

My new job required me to travel around North Dakota, and so I had a chance to stop into the county courthouses on my journeys. I took a copy of my Stud Book with me, and examined the voting records in every county election office of anyone who had voted with an absentee ballot who were also named in the Stud Book. I put a red dot beside every one of those.

I was not overly surprised when names started popping up with both a red And a green dot. These represented people who voted twice in that election – once on campus and also by absentee in their home town. This was 1976 – it was a federal election. This was also Voter Fraud – a federal crime.

I didn't quite get to all the county seats, and stopped counting when I had documented that at least 240 NDSU students had voted twice. It was fully documentable – all the proof was there in plain sight to anyone who cared to look.

I was, at that point, the only one who did.

It was the summer of 1977. The legislative session had already come and gone. The fellow who won the election was closely tied to NDSU through the Alumni Association, the Team Makers and via one of the local fraternities.

A little sleuthing revealed the role of the fraternity in urging its members and others to double-vote that year, and they assured those they recruited that "no one will ever know."

So there I was – with some damning incontrovertible evidence fully in hand. What to do?

While in Bismarck, I took it to several people in the Democratic Party, seeking guidance on how to proceed, if at all. Their response was revealing:

Even though what I was claiming was provable, it would nevertheless cause a great political upset in the state, and would quite likely end up with a requirement for voter registration rather than the current system. That was a more important political outcome than getting the election process correct would be, so they urged me just to let it go.

So much for all that Rising Political Star stuff. Lesson well learned.

I told a reporter friend about it, and he said he would report the story if I filed the federal criminal complaint, but that he worked for the Fargo Forum, and it wasn't terribly interested in initiating the story.

I was still unconvinced. This was, to my belief, just So Egregious a Wrong that it had to be righted, and the only way it could be righted would be for me to take my evidence to the U.S. Attorney, and file a federal criminal complain against – at that point – some 240 young people who were obviously so naïve that they figured such a thing could never be found out.

But then I got the best advice, from a dear friend – Pat Geston Hansen. She had been my art teacher in Eighth grade at Ben Franklin, my freshman composition professor at NDSU in 1962-1963, and my advanced composition professor at NDSU later on.

I was, to be honest, somewhere between crushed-slash-disappointed and red-hot angry. I didn't mind losing all that much, but to lose This way was infuriating. I had pretty much decided to go ahead and file the complaint, watch while the investigation proved the allegation was correct, and let the chips fall where they might.

Pat talked me out of it. She reminded me that my heart really wasn't in it in the first place, that really there was No way of proving beyond any reasonable doubt that all of those double-voters had voted for my opponent, when they might have easily have voted for me as well to some degree. Though I could prove they had committed a federal crime, it would do nothing to reverse the outcome of the election itself.

But more importantly, she reminded me, I would be creating a large group of people with a criminal record. These were people I knew, people scarce ten years younger than I, people just starting out on making their own way into the world. Having a criminal record would create a lot of problems that

245

even though they had acted improperly and stupidly, nevertheless they probably really didn't deserve.

She advised me just to let it go.

That's where I finally ended up.

That was my parting political gift to the state, but more importantly, to those who were gullible and naïve enough to believe that what they did couldn't be noticed. It could indeed. There was no widespread and costly investigation, no trials and plea bargains, no deep personal sense of embarrassment to be experienced thereafter.

It is now coming up on fifty years later. Most of those involved are now in their 60s and have lived full and good lives for the most part. They may not even remember this smallish act that seemed like a mere prank at the time. Perhaps they have learned a lesson, though, but then in today's heated political climate, perhaps not. I hope no one has done the same thing since, but I have no way of knowing, and it no longer matters.

I have never publicly told this story before. The statute of limitations has long since run out and I trust the records to substantiate the actions have long since been destroyed. I burned the Stud Book I kept about fifteen years ago.

I think I did the right thing. Reluctantly, I will admit.

But that's what really happened.

I have not since seriously run for any office. I have several times filed for office when someone is running unopposed in a race in which the opposing party failed in its duty to offer voters a choice of candidates. I believe that's simply wrong. I haven't done any serious fundraising on my own behalf. I haven't sucked up to anyone seeking some special treatment by investing in a candidate.

I make no claim to any personal moral uprightness in all of that. As Clint Eastwood said in one of his Dirty Harry movies,

"A man's Got to know his limitations." He said that just after blowing his nemesis, Briggs, to smithereens with a car bomb.

I know mine. Being a Politician is beyond them.

After the election loss in 1976, Cal Olsen, formerly of The Forum and then working for Prairie Public Television, did a story on The Losers. I was one of the interviewees. I said in that interview that Nothing is quite so out of date as last year's politician.

I also mentioned there were some other things I was considering that might still have a public impact.

And there were.

One, in particular, was right around the corner.

43.

The Other Best Thing

As I consider some of the things I was involved with during my life, I smile at this one, and get a very deep sense of satisfaction.

This is the story of the second time I was privileged to Do Good on a large scale. I had taken a position as Executive Director of a non-profit that dealt with developmentally disabled people, and had managed to form a coalition of similar non-profit groups. It was my hope that rather than each of us being small, and competing for funds, we could cooperate on mutually desirable goals in our small state, and perhaps do something useful and positive.

While in the legislature, we had passed an appropriation for a new administration building at the Grafton State School. That was the institution where developmentally disabled people were kept and supposedly educated. On a trip to the school, it struck me that we had made the administrators quite comfortable with new air conditioned offices, but that what I was allowed to see in the patient wards was nowhere near as appropriate.

So the non-profit several groups prevailed on a fellow from Cornell University to come to Grafton and take a tour and report on what he saw. It was by no means a thorough and exhaustive study of the facility. It was never meant to be. What he saw was more than sufficient to have the entire institution become subject to the harsh light of public scrutiny and for us to describe it as a "hellhole" and to demand improvements at least, and a different way of dealing with developmentally disabled individuals across the entire state.

I was chosen to be the point person in the first blast of statewide publicity releasing the report. Maura Jones, then the director of the local Association for Retarded Citizens (its name at the time – it has since changed a couple of times) chartered a plane and several of us flew to Bismarck, Minot, Grand Forks and finally Fargo to hold a series of press conferences all on the same day.

The public reaction was sharply divided and mostly negative initially. There were those who believed what we said, and there were those who largely thought it didn't really matter, that "Those People" didn't need much better than they had.

The state agencies involved got an advanced case of The Vapors about the whole thing. How Dare We criticize their best efforts to do right by these unfortunate residents? Why, the staff were Caring People and just Loved those individuals they were responsible for!

The saddest group in opposition we heard from were those who had placed their children at Grafton in all good faith, believing what they were told, and trusting that things were as good as could be. There was a certain level of desperation in all of that – they had no other real choice, and so could not come to believe that what they were most familiar and even comfortable with was simply not appropriate. Worse, though, they feared that if the institution closed, the children would be returned to them – and that was simply unthinkable.

It was a hard time to get through. The letters to local papers across the state were vehement, and mostly critical. As the point person in the initial PR efforts, I felt like I was on the downwind edge of a "shit storm" many times. I got phone calls at home, threatening letters at the office, was called out publicly many times over. I did interviews with television and radio stations across the state, and the reporters (who were largely clueless but had to report Something) were neither knowledgeable nor frankly even familiar with the issue.

There were several times when the folks in the coalition were most frustrated, and were nearly prepared to back away from the whole thing. It took considerable effort to keep them going in the same direction, and focused on the same goal.

The early part of the process culminated in a joint legislative hearing – the appropriate committees and members of Both houses of the state legislature would come together to hash this thing out in its entirety.

Prior to that hearing, a state official came to me to say that I should find a way to place the blame on the Republicans. The governor was a Democrat, the previous governor had also been a Democrat, and though no Democrat had offered to remediate the situation in previous legislative sessions, nevertheless the Republicans had been in charge of the legislature and so the blame should properly fall on them.

I refused to do that, point blank. Having no longer any political aspirations myself, and having no particular party allegiance, I simply said that Both of the parties had failed in their duty to the developmentally disabled community. So far as I was concerned I was going to take dead aim at both sides equally. Because both deserved it.

The joint legislative hearing was fascinating. The head of the Grafton State School gave an impassioned defense of the place, noting – quite correctly – that he and his staff had been doing the very best they could with what they had been provided. In my testimony, before a quite hostile panel, I merely said that what the school had been provided with was not nearly enough, and that the legislature should make it a very high priority to remediate the huge problems in upcoming sessions.

One of the Senators demanded to know whether my organization was planning to sue the state. Such class action lawsuits were, at the time, the main way that improvements in such state institutions got accomplished over generally intransigent and uncooperative state governments.

I replied, quite sincerely, that No – My organization was not planning to sue anyone. I just wanted the situation to be corrected.

That was a truthful statement. My organization was not planning on launching a class-action lawsuit. But…I knew which organization Was planning to do that. He didn't ask, so I didn't say.

The part I played was to, as some might call it, plough the ground or perhaps prepare the battlefield, if one wishes to use military parlance. There was a need to change public perception and opinion across the entire state before any lawsuit could even start, much less be successful. I knew coming into it that I would be the focus of a blast of negative publicity, and that I would just have to hang on while it blew through. It did. Other people began to visit Grafton, and reporters began to do longer, more thorough stories about its all-too-obvious deficiencies and shortcomings. Over time, public perception Did change, public opinion went the other way and the stage was set for the solution to be implemented.

The legislature was given its chance to fix things. It failed.

So in the fullness of time, the class action lawsuit was filed, and the then very young new attorney handling it became the focus of public attention. I got to back away from the uncomfortable but necessary flack I had been taking, and return

251

once again to leading a far more normal sort of life, well out of the public eye.

The lawsuit was successful. It probably cost the state something over $300 million before it was over. A network of local group homes, with more competent staff, proper medical treatment, appropriate therapies and better integration with local communities was developed. The Grafton State School was radically downsized in favor of community-based facilities that could and did do a better job.

I have a large binder of media clippings from the time that show how the entire matter began, was developed, and finally ended. I haven't looked through it in years – it's now history. But every now and then, as I consider some of the things I was involved with during my life, I smile at this one, and get a very deep sense of satisfaction.

44.

Zs

When I left Fargo in October 1980,
I pointed the Black Pearl east.

My wife and I had owned a lot of different cars over the years, but we'd kept the black-on-black Corvair convertible we'd started dating in.

Over the years, I'd added several more Covairs to the collection, all 1966s – a turbocharged coupe and convertible, and a 4-carb coupe. All Corsas. And a 4-carb Monza with factory a/c. And a Yenko Stinger #043.

Six of them in all, simultaneously. Those were excessive, no question. But... they didn't Get Girls. Therefore permissible.

When the lead went out of gasoline, I couldn't afford to convert all those heads to hardened valve seats, so I sold the Corvairs piecemeal. The hardest sale was the black convertible – to a guy from Jamestown, ND. In retrospect, over my lifetime since, that's the car I miss more than any other. Even more than the Corvette – and I miss that one too.

When I sold the Corvairs, I bought the first of two Datsun 280Zs.

It was a 1975 Datsun 280Z, which I picked up for $3500. Metallic copper, 4-speed, fuel injected, reliable, not too pricey. Nice to drive, though. I put an air dam on the front, headlight covers and a rear spoiler on the back.

A good friend said if I ever found another, he'd like to buy it. I found a beauty out by Detroit Lakes, and showed it to him. Same color, 1976, only with an 8-track tape deck. He really wanted it. His wife said No. So much for that.

My wife, however, came out of the house, saw the car and asked me if it was a good one. I allowed as to how Yes – it was. She wrote a check for $4300 and bought it on the spot.

Now picture this: We had *matching* 280Zs. That's about as Yuppy as one might ever imagine, though I don't recall the term was in vogue at the time. But it was a Style Statement, no question. She drove it for years, and after she moved to Minneapolis, it finally recycled itself back into the rust from which it had come.

I bought my second Z – a '78 "Black Pearl," in 1978. That year, Nissan/Datsun did a test market of the 280Z. They had never made one in any black color previously, and so did a small series of cars in Nissan Paint Code 638 – Black Pearl Metallic. Each dealer got one and only one – so there were 858 made. Amongst Z aficionados, these are known as the Black Pearls – no connection to the pirate movies.

The circumstances of that purchase were a little flakey. When I bought it, I still owned the 1975. But a friend in Dickinson wanted to buy that one for his wife, so I bought the Black Pearl and drove it down into the basement of the old Overvold Motors garage, when it was located on Fifth Street and Fourth Avenue, and hid it underground. Didn't tell my wife what I'd done. Got the other one sold and Then I told her.

She figured out what I'd done and was Not happy I hadn't told her. Ah, well – the marriage was ending anyway. We both sort of knew that, and there's only so much harm that could have arisen.

I still own the Black Pearl – have for 36 years. It's the car that brought my current wife and me together. Redid it several years back, have taken it to shows and have well over a dozen trophies.

But there remains that piece of my memory that can still see and feel how it was to drive that black Corvair convertible. If I could find it, I'd buy it back, put it right and wouldn't change a thing from when it was "new" to me.

The memory is all wrapped up in that whole Viet Nam thing and the way I thought about it during 1968. I suspect that memory will never leave me, even when I go to The Home.

When I finally left Fargo for good, in October 1980, I pointed the Black Pearl east. The divorce papers were filed, an agreement on finances made, and it was time to get on with the rest of my life.

PART VI

45.

We're Talking Turkey

"Nice big bird," said Mom.

It started in July with a local Fargo grocery store promotion. "How big is this turkey?" the ads asked. Guesses ran to 30 pounds or so.

Actually it was just a tad over 45 pounds. This was, you may be assured, a *large* turkey. But in July, no one wanted a very large turkey, so the grocer put it in the freezer till a more auspicious time.

It came to pass that Mom was in the store just before Thanksgiving. Mom was a naturally talkative person, and she struck up a conversation with the butcher at the counter.

"I need kind of a big turkey for my family," said Mom.

To which the butcher replied, "Well, if you are looking for a Big Turkey, I may have just the thing." And he hauled out the 45-pound bird for Mom.

"Nice big bird," said Mom, "but it would cost far too much for my fixed income budget."

"Here's the deal," said the friendly butcher. "I can't move this bird at all at the usual price. No one wants a bird this big, so tell you what I'll do. I'll sell you this turkey for 49 cents a pound."

Mom, who was nobody's fool, thought that such a purchase would be entirely reasonable. After all, less than twenty bucks or so for a really BIG turkey would be a reasonable price. And besides, of such stuff are Family Legends made. Little did she know.

"Sold," said Mom.

There was a problem. Mom was 70, and though she lived only about a block from the store, getting The Bird home was No Easy Thing. Mom didn't drive. Ever.

So, she hiked back to her place and got a baby buggy. Not one of your "stroller" contraptions – this was a genuine old-style baby buggy, with a deep space that could easily hold a toddler.

Or a 45 pound turkey.

"Wrap that turkey up completely," said Mom to the butcher. "I don't want anyone to think I am taking a dead turkey for a walk." Which he did. Mom took the turkey back to her place in the baby buggy.

It took full four days to thaw.

I showed up in Fargo two days early, and Mom was all a-twitter with ideas for how to put on a family dinner *tour-de-force*. We are talking *major* stuffing here. So, off we went to the various stores to purchase dinner-making stuff.

Allow me to note something important: No One – anywhere – makes a roasting bag to handle a 45-pound turkey. Few roasting pans can handle it either. We bought one of those nifty open aluminum roasting pans, figuring to cover the bird with, oh, an acre or so of aluminum foil. But there were some interesting engineering problems to deal with. Like how to lift it.

"No problem," said Mom, "we'll just get some cheesecloth, wrap the bird in a kind of sling, and lift it that way."

260

Elegant solution. Mom had clearly missed her true calling as an engineer.

And so, the Night Before, figuring we'd need a really long cooking time, we stuffed, slung, positioned, covered, vented the bird, and popped it in the oven at about 1:30 a.m.

And so to bed, for a long winter's nap.

Wrong. At 3:15 a.m., I heard Mom calling my name.

You must understand, when things are going well, I am "Don" to everyone, including Mom. When that was not the case, I became "Donald."

Mom had a special way of saying Donald.

"Donald," she said, "Oh, *Donald!*"

I answered groggily. "What? Whatsamatter?" I knew Mom, and waking folks at 3:15 a.m. was just not her style.

"Donald," she said, "*we* have a problem."

"What," I responded, "problem do We have?"

"Our Turkey is running over," said Mom. (The shift from "the" turkey to "our" turkey was subtly done, in retrospect. At the time, it was effective. This was now a Truly Joint Crisis.)

For those who do not quite comprehend the problem, turkeys, in the process of cooking, release large quantities of juices, which, with normal birds, later becomes gravy. For this bird, it had become a flood, and had overflowed the all-too-shallow roasting pan into the bottom of a hot oven.

Smoke. Small apartment. Smoke detectors suddenly blaring at 3:16 a.m., roughly corresponding to opening the oven door. And cleaning turkey juices from the bottom of a hot oven at 3:19 a.m. is No Easy Thing, I assure you. Many towels, not of the paper variety. Some other cloth materials I still do not recognize. Mom was ready for any crisis of spill, apparently.

It finally got cleaned up. The towels got put in the washer at about 3:30 a.m., the fan blew the smoke out of the apartment.

The smoke detectors got reset, and so to bed, for a slightly shorter winter's nap than originally planned

Wrong again.

The turkey overflowed – again – at 5:20 a.m. Same scenario, in all relevant ways.

This time, we tried to suck up some of the juices from the roaster, but the turkey baster bulb was bad, and wouldn't create a vacuum. Smoke alarms, much general good-natured grousing, and Mom standing around saying gratuitous things like "If I had known this would happen, I never would have bought that damned turkey."

Now, there is just no way an eldest son can respond to that, other than with variations on a theme of, "Oh, it's all right, Mom. This is just Another Neat Adventure on the Road of Life, and Someday We'll All Laugh At This Together."

Mom wasn't buying it. This was not Meaningful Family Interaction. This was Crisis Management.

So we each played our predestined roles, and eventually it was cleaned up.

Just in time, for it was coming up on 7:00 a.m., time to shower and shave and get ready for the siblings and grandchildren to arrive.

By about 11:30 a.m., the tiny kitchen was crowded with Mom and the two sisters, moving in a mysterious choreography, getting in each other's way, using the Very Dish That I Needed for things like glorified rice and other holiday foods, and the general buzz of Big Holiday Meal Preparation.*

When the time came to lift the bird, out it came in Mom's cheesecloth sling, just as nice as you please. It looked like something out of a Norman Rockwell painting on its platter, all

---

* The two sisters were Lois and Maureen, mom's two youngest children. Lois was Dad's last child, and Maureen was Martin Mickelson's, whom Mom had married a few years after Dad died.

golden brown, crispy skinned, with the dark meat just beginning to flake on the legs. And the smell was amazing!

Much frenetic activity followed, including the required Making of the Gravy from what remained of the copious turkey juices now resting in the bottom of the pan.

Mom was never one of your cornstarch gravy people. She did a flour paste, mixing it thoroughly and putting it in a bowl, thereafter to be stirred into the gravy juices for several minutes, and it really was quite wonderful.

I have to tell you, I was standing right there, and I don't know how it happened. But somehow, the white glass bowl with the flour/water mixture in it ended up on top of the stove. On a burner. Which was on. High! The bowl was opaque white glass, not Pyrex, and not made for this kind of insult.

The bowl exploded.

I don't mean cracked and fell apart, I mean "exploded," with a loud bang, throwing waist-high glass splinters mixed with flour and water all around the kitchen, including onto the aforementioned hot burner, which promptly gave off a cloud of smoke, setting off the aforementioned smoke alarms again, which caused the smallest children to panic and cry – well, you get the idea.

I went into crisis intervention mode and:

       a. turned off the burner
       b. threw everyone out of the kitchen
       c. disconnected the smoke alarm
       d. opened the windows
       e. started to clean up the mess

Mom, meanwhile, had been standing there all this time, watching this happen with an air of almost mystic detachment. I was looking directly at her when she recovered her poise.

263

"Damn," said Mom, "that was my last flour. I'll have to go to the store and get some more." She put her coat on and out the door she went.

Leaving yours truly to once again reorganize the scene. And when she got back with flour, about 15 minutes later, all was again In Order, and the day progressed more or less uneventfully.

The dinner was magnificent! The quantity and quality of the leftovers was astonishing. It was, in every possible way, An Event of Significance.

But it was Not Yet Over.

The Sisters took over the kitchen, cleaning everything up and generally fulfilling the role of Dutiful Daughters (I had already fulfilled the role of Dutiful Son for most of the previous night), packing the dishwasher, putting stuff away, and Turning On the Self-Cleaning Oven.

For those not familiar with this technology, Self-Cleaning Ovens heat themselves up to a really high temperature, lock themselves (this is important) with a solenoid so that no one can open them, then heat *way* up – far hotter than the 500-degree Fahrenheit cooking temperature limit – and literally burn the stuff off the inside, reducing it to a fine ash that can easily be wiped out or even sucked out with a small vacuum cleaner.

Remember the aforementioned overflowing turkey juice?

There was still a fair amount of it left on the bottom of the oven.

We had not gotten around to sponging it out, and a late-arriving sister didn't know that a final cleanup needed to be done.

So now the oven was **really hot** and **locked** with a plentiful supply of turkey juice on the bottom; and of course, it had a vent for excess heat.

Smoke!

264

Not just a little smoke; we are talking SMOKE here – billows of smoke, clouds of acrid smoke, really *serious* smoke.

And the aforementioned smoke alarms, causing little children to panic and cry.

Pandemonium once again!

Open windows, and smoke billows out. Open doors to hallway, and smoke fills the entire apartment complex. Which, of course, has its own smoke alarms and automatic fire department call relays.

And we can't open the damned oven!

So, more smoke, more alarms and neighbors with shouts of, "Call the fire department!"

And a general Hue and Cry, much confusion, laughter, embarrassment and all the other Holiday Emotions, just more acute than usual.

We put fans in the windows, and assured everyone that The Situation is Temporary and Really Under Control. Mom moved wraith-like through it all, and kept saying "Boy, we're going to remember this one for a long time."

In due time, the smoke cleared, folks all went home, and the Holiday turned out to be a great success. Everyone was tired and laughing, with kids exhausted from the emotional roller-coaster.

It was great!

I hope all yours can be as great, though perhaps not in quite the same way.

For which You May Be Truly Thankful.

46.

John Hildreth

A Fargo thread wraps around the world.

In the 1950s, teachers were women. Period. Men – Real Men – weren't teachers. They did other things. They were school principals, or Phy Ed instructors (which weren't really Teachers as the term was understood at the time).

As a result, the role models for education professionals tended to be women. Make no mistake, there were some truly Great female teachers. But in retrospect, the lack of male teachers was somewhat unfortunate for boys – the role models available were constricted.

I got my first male teacher in Eighth grade at Ben Franklin Junior High School, over on Eighth Street North just north of where Shanley High School was at the time. John Hildreth taught Eighth grade English, and getting him as a teacher was something quite new.

For one thing, his attitude toward the boys in the class was, well, Different from the women teachers I had previously experienced. He seemed more tolerant of the things boys did, perhaps somewhat amused. Behaviors that would elicit a frown from the women in earlier years would like as not get a bemused smile from John, and he'd guide that boyish enthusiasm and energy back into constructive activities.

For me, that meant actually Doing the work and applying myself with some effort. That was different from my experience the previous year with Mrs. South, who acted as though all boys were mostly a bother, and who spoke to us in a tone and manner as though we were all still in first grade.

I can recall when Hildreth first introduced us to sentence diagramming – which is now as I understand it something passé in English education – he explained it more as a puzzle to be solved than as a task to do. That just made it better and more interesting. It wasn't my favorite activity, certainly, but it was better than it had been before.

John drove a 1953 Studebaker coupe – one of the Raymond Loewy-designed (famous for designing the Coca-Cola bottle and later the Studebaker Avanti) beautiful little low-slung cars. It was white, with plain (perhaps Moon) hubcaps. That design has come down to auto buffs – and I am one of those – as one of The iconic American car designs. If memory serves, John's car was actually a "Studillac" – a Studebaker with a Cadillac V-8 in it, which was itself somewhat unusual at the time, and is a matter of great interest among car collectors now. There weren't many made, and most have disappeared.

For all the novelty having Hildreth as a teacher involved, still and all he was a teacher. There were many such, and after leaving Eighth grade, there were other male teachers, usually in the Science classes, and I sort of lost track of John for some years.

When I got back from Viet Nam in 1968, I was active in the YMCA at NDSU. Hildreth owned a small house just down the street from the small ranch-style house that the YMCA operated out of at the time. I saw him walking on the street one day, and stopped to talk. Over the ensuing couple of years, we had the chance to chat from time to time and he seemed interested how I had grown and changed. It was nice to see him as an Actual Person, outside the role of teacher. It's not clear how that realization grows on someone.

It was sometime in 1971, if memory serves, that John called me on the phone and asked if I would come by. He said he had something to give me. I had just No idea what it might be, but I went.

When I came in, he told me that as a kid, his grandfather had given him an old and very curious map. It was printed on tissue paper, dated 1893, the fading colors were hand-brushed. It was folded up, as it had been kept pressed inside a large book for decades, and it was very fragile. He opened it carefully on a table so I could see it.

It was quite the thing!

As a preacher's kid myself, I had more than a passing knowledge of scripture, and by that time, as a practicing skeptic, I had become somewhat amused at the odd ways in which the True Believers at various times presented their beliefs to everyone else as Revealed Truth. Knowing something about the history of science, I knew that the time the map was published was also the time of the Michelson-Morley experiments. Those were famous in that they seemed, at the time, to show that the earth was standing still in the firmament of heaven, and was in fact the center of the universe. (Those experiments were shown to be incorrect later, for various reasons that are not germane to this discussion.)

The map was entitled "The Square and Stationary Earth" and was a fanciful attempt to bolster that core idea – that the earth really is stationary, and square – by using scriptural references. It claimed "This Map is the Bible Map of the World" and went about listing all the quotes in the Bible it was drawn from, summing up with:

Send 25 cents to the Author, Prof. Orlando Ferguson, for a book explaining this Square and Stationary Earth. It Knocks the Globe Theory Clean Out. It will Teach You How to Foretell Eclipses. It is Worth its Weight in Gold.

The map was drawn in 3D showing the earth shaped like an extra-thick pizza box with a shallow roulette wheel-like indentation in the center. It was an interesting piece, but at the time I found it curious, not particularly compelling. It was merely an advertising flyer, to be handed out free, to elicit interest in the book "Professor Ferguson" was selling for the princely sum of 25 cents. It was a throwaway.*

Somehow it had survived nearly 80 years in pretty good condition.

When John gave it to me, he said that he'd kept it all these years, and wanted to give it to me because "You are the one person I thought would really appreciate it for what it really is." I'm pleased he felt that. I suspect that someone else might not have appreciated it in its proper historical context, and it would have been discarded as just another strange curiosity. I really valued it. It spoke to me about matters I thought were more important than they seemed.

I took it, thanked John and put it with my collection of other curious things, and for some 14 years or so didn't give it much more thought. I would pull it out from time to time to show to friends, mostly as a means of demonstrating how religious fervor could lead to some quite amusing misperceptions of the true state of nature in many quite fascinating ways.

About 1985 or so, I had it framed so it could be hung on a wall. It wasn't properly "conserved," but at least it wasn't subject

---

* You can see the map John gave me by doing an Internet search of "Square and Stationary Earth." **Spoiler Alert:** Don't read any of the articles associated with the map before you finish the story you're reading here.

to constant handling, folding and unfolding, which would damage it over time. I would look at it daily. One day I got to wondering if the book itself had survived. I looked for it on line, but never found anything other than a reference that the book had existed. There were apparently none available, either for sale or even just for reference.

John died – I don't remember when. I do remember that I felt some sorrow for the passing of another significant figure in my life, but he wasn't the first and wouldn't be the last. And I had that great memento from him.

Sometime about 2005, by that time living in Oregon, I had it reframed, this time, properly – by a conservator of old paper. It was put on acid-free paper, carefully mounted so it couldn't touch glass and placed in a sealed frame so it wouldn't deteriorate any further. It was hung on the wall of our family room, and friends who saw it remarked on its uniqueness quite often. I was always pleased to tell its story and put the map itself into its proper historical context. In that process, I had a full-size true color digital copy of it made, just for future reference.

A couple of years later, I got to thinking about the map itself, rather than the book it was promoting. I commenced a search to see if it had been mentioned anywhere on line. (By that time, the sum of human knowledge was fast going on line, so I figured that I might find it.) I found one – in a museum in Hot Springs, South Dakota, the town where Orlando Ferguson had come up with it. There was a photo of it taken by a tourist who had come through the museum and seen it, and it looked to be in pretty sorry shape.

In my searches, I ran across a great grand-niece of Ferguson's. She had asked if anyone out there had any information about him, and that somehow in the family's lore he had become known as "Flat Earth Ferguson," but she didn't know why.

I did know why, and I got in touch with her and told her. I also made her a full-size copy and gave it to her so she could see it. She was already in her 80s, and said she was grateful to have the mystery finally revealed.

A couple more years of on and off searching through the Internet, and one day it finally came to me:

I have, perhaps, the Only one of these maps in the world still in good condition.

What to do?

I did find a collector's market for old unique maps. None of those sites had one of these. The rarer the map, the more valuable it was. My wife and I thought about selling it, but that action seemed somehow to violate John's spirit. Treating this gift as something to be sold seemed inappropriate.

We decided that perhaps we should donate it to a museum instead. So I got in touch with the Smithsonian Museum to see if it would be at all interested in this unique piece of Americana. But the response from them was discouraging – No, they were not interested. Just didn't do that sort of thing. But perhaps if I contacted the Library of Congress.

So I did. Found the curator of the Library's map collection – a fellow named Robert Morris. I sent him an e-mail with a scan of the map itself, and asked if the Library of Congress might perhaps already have a copy of it, but that if it did not, I would happily donate ours.

It just seemed to my wife and me that the nation should have this memorabilia of a particular time, place and sensibility, rather than some private collector who might lock it away unseen. John would have been both amused and gratified. Since it was his personal gift to me, it wasn't as though I had more than four or five hundred dollars invested in it.

A week or so later, I got a reply. No – the Library of Congress did Not have a copy of that map among its 5 million or so maps. In fact, it was not even aware that such a map actually existed! Yes, it would be Most pleased to accept the map as a donation.

As it turns out, the period around 1890 was rife with a lot of strange theories about what the earth really looked like, whether or not earth was really the center of the universe, how light propagated through the aether (later found not to exist at all, but at the time, predating Einstein, no one knew how that whole light thing actually worked) and those who devoutly espoused religious thought weighed in with their source of Revealed Truth, so the scriptural debate was on. There were a lot of words, but few actual maps of what participants thought the world actually looked like were ever published, and fewer survived. John's map was rare indeed!

The Library of Congress said they would send a truck to wrap it properly and ship it to DC. A formal presentation ceremony was arranged to take place at the Library of Congress, which was duly reported by the news media.

The resulting media whirlwind was astonishing. The map got national and world-wide publicity. Friends in England sent me links to articles in English newspapers, and a little searching showed articles from India, Russia, China and even Viet Nam. They included pictures of the map as a rare curiosity.

As a result, two more copies of the map showed up – but both in pretty sad shape. One had been glued to a nylon net, which meant that for all practical purposes it had been severely damaged. One had been taken from a trunk in a barn but was missing a large chunk. The one in Hot Springs had been glued to a piece of cardboard, and was deteriorating rapidly. Mine was original and still in pretty good shape, properly conserved so it would last indefinitely.

272

The small ceremony was very nice. Emissaries from several congresscritters attended, and Senator Jeff Merkely from Oregon showed up in person, surprising me by asking some intelligent questions. He or his staff had done their homework.

My wife and I were given a tour of the vault, where we saw other maps from other interesting people, including one hand-drawn by George Washington, titled "My Farm." Morris told us that map was 250 years old and still in good shape. Ours was 125 years old, and when it was as old as GW's map, it would still be in good shape, and still have our name on it.

We don't have any friends who have their names on an exhibit in the Library of Congress. We are both somewhat proud and somewhat humbled at all of that.

In the short-lived spate of online enthusiasm about the map, we had several folks suggest that we use the image on a T-shirt, and they offered to pay us a royalty to do so. But as far as we're concerned, the map belongs to the Library of Congress, and if it can make a few bucks from selling that image, fine by us. We're not about to turn it into a money-making event on our own behalf. We let that one go.

To take the IRS tax deduction, we had to have it appraised. The appraiser we hired to do that came back with the report that he couldn't come up with a value on it. There had never been one sold at auction, and that it was so rare that there was no market to discuss. He said a collector might well pay well into six figures for it, but that the IRS would accept a $5,000 appraisal for tax purposes without further question. So that's the figure we used.

On the History.com blog, one of the commenters noted that this sort of thing is the very Stuff of History, and not just a tale about it. We like that too. It is exactly that.

In May 2012, my wife and I drove a 1959 Cadillac from the Left Coast to deliver that car to a friend in northern Minnesota.

En route, we stopped in to visit the county museum in Hot Springs, South Dakota, where another copy of the map was still on display. Serendipitously once again, they had been searching for the original book. In a box in the local library, folks in Hot Springs had found an unblemished untouched original copy of the book. The places where the pages had been joined together in printing had not even been cut apart - it was that original. They didn't care to sell it to me (I did offer) but they made an archival quality pdf of it, and put that on a digital disc. The book is mostly a religious rant. Turns out Orlando Ferguson didn't think very highly of most folks, and said so quite vehemently.

My wife and I also visited the local cemetery in Hot Springs, and to our considerable delight, found the Ferguson family gravesite plot, with Orlando's name clearly visible on the stone. I took some photos of that.

After returning from the trip, I took the digital copy of the book and the photos and transmitted them to the Library of Congress, along with three copies of Orlando Ferguson's obituary from local newspapers at the time. In my letter of transmittal, I noted that the Library of Congress now had All the available information that could be gotten on a matter of No particular significance at all.

We left it at that.

So it was that John Hildreth, a junior high English teacher in Fargo, made a significant impression on my life at the time. Neither of us had any idea what, if anything, would come of it. The later adult friendship that was formed would have been Nice all on its own, and his small gift just something to remember with a smile.

John never lived to know all the great fun that gift generated decades later. I'd like to think that he would have found it most enjoyable indeed.

Once again, one of those early Fargo threads came back in later life, and for a brief time, generated some considerable interest far beyond where anyone would have guessed it might go. I continue to be grateful for that, and am pleased that John's name will be remembered, even in this small way.

47.

Taking Down Names

and Knitting

There are those people who, as they age,
fade gently into that good night.
Not Mom.

Complicated woman, Mom.

She made friends easily, but by the time she died she had "snotted off" every one of them, to the point where most refused to have anything to do with her. She was so unremittingly critical, brooking no human failings whatsoever, that eventually they couldn't stand being around her.

It took her family, as well, some considerable work to remain on good terms. Coming from a defiantly anti-Papist family (we have some of her grandfather's writings against the Roman Catholics in an old railway journal that he kept) she harbored a virulent hatred of Catholics. She was convinced that there was always some hanky-panky going on, but thought it was between priests and nuns – and said so to anyone who was unfortunate enough to be around when she launched into that discussion. (When the church's modern sex scandal began to become known, she had the personal satisfaction of being able to say "I told you so" to those who had earlier suggested she was a bit over the top on any of that.)

I wish we had been better able to stay on good terms as she grew older, but she got crossways with my wife – a recovering Catholic – during a visit once. When my wife suggested, quite reasonably, that she not go there, Mom went non-linear immediately. I stood by my wife – that's what husbands do – and Mom took it personally. Things were never quite the same after that.

But there was a fascinating twist to all this. Though Mom had difficulty finding a way to be on good terms with anyone whose life was better than hers, or was going better than hers, if by some mischance someone else's life took a downward turn, Mom's treatment of them did an immediate 180. It was almost as though she had an odd form of what the Germans call "schadenfreude" – a sort of personal pleasure at someone else's misfortune, because they were now suddenly worse off than she was.

I saw it happen a couple of times with estranged friends. If they got sick or were injured, Mom could make up with them overnight and would, during such periods, be entirely solicitous and helpful. Her friends found this mildly schizophrenic – and perhaps it was.

I saw it in my own family when my wife was diagnosed with very early stage breast cancer. The two of us were devastated! The mammogram was on Monday, the biopsy was on Tuesday and the lumpectomy was on Friday. Mom took the diagnosis in stride. OK – my wife had breast cancer. That meant that even if she was a Catholic, she was suddenly worth humane treatment from that point onward.

After the surgery, Mom called Kathy several times to inquire how she was. She also spoke with me, and was especially attentive to the chemotherapy regimen. My wife had decided to go with the harder of two choices – a worse time in chemo, but a better chance of beating it. It was not only hard, it nearly killed her! Twice!

Mom really couldn't do all that much, and I wasn't about to allow her to visit while my wife's immune system crashed from the chemo. But she did what she could from Fargo, knitting my wife "cancer hats" for her to wear after her hair all came out. In the end, about six of them – each a work of art all on its own. Obviously lovingly done, with fine needles, softest wool and patterns knitted into them. They remain both a fond possession and a memory of something special that we prefer to remember.

Which is a longish way of getting around to another knitting-related story about Mom, but one with a larger sort of community impact.

*   *   *

Mom was never one to prefer getting angry over getting even. The latter was Far better, in her mind.

On a visit to the Red River Valley State Fair one year, Mom went by the knitting exhibit which had mostly been entered by a local knitting club. She was not, truth be told, all that terribly impressed by the winners. She said that she could do, and had done, much better than that. The story was never quite clear, but she may have said that within earshot of one of the knitting club people at the display. Words may have been exchanged. Upshot: She came home from the Fair determined to enter some of her knitting. She had been challenged.

What the challenger didn't know was that since before I was born, Mom was a knitter.

She knitted everything – mittens, socks, scarves, sweaters and most especially what she called a Baby Layette. That was a little knitted cap (with a satin rosette on each side), a matching sweater, little booties for the feet and an infant blanket. They all matched wool colors. They had patterns knitted into them, a different pattern for each kid.

She did that for every one of her own six, as well as gifts for other children of friends and relatives over the years. It got to the point where she really didn't need the knitting pattern books she had purchased in 1943 – she could do them nearly by memory.

So the following year, she made and entered one of those layette assemblies into the contest. Worked on it for several months. Used the smallest needles available with fine and even stitches. Used real wool – Mom was never fond of the acrylics.

She won the contest that year, hands down. It wasn't even Close in the judging, so I was told by Someone Who Knew.

But then… it started. The Ladies of the Knitting Club were apparently not terribly complimentary to her when she went to pick up the ribbon. I have No idea who these Ladies were or are – this was not my fight. It was hers alone, and she was Bound to have it. But forever after, Mom called them "the old biddies." She felt slighted – which was Never the way to treat Mom. Apparently the members of the local knitting group had become annually accustomed to sharing the ribbons among themselves, and they were mildly resentful of some lone knitter dropping in out of nowhere and walking away with the top prize.

So rather than have the personal pleasure of a straight-up win, Mom now had a battle on her hands. Being who she was, she got into the fray with a vengeance. And relish.

As a kid, Mom had been fascinated by the Dionne Quintuplets – five young girls conceived without the aid of fertility treatments. They were a *cause célèbre* in Canada (they were Canadian, so there was a nationalistic thing going on as well) for years, and the magazines in the U.S. and Canada followed them for decades.

Somewhere, Mom found five identical Dionne Quintuplet dolls, and she got straightaway to work. For the rest of the year, Mom knitted up a storm! The intention was to make five identical layettes – one for each of the dolls – but in a different color for each. Cap, booties, sweater and blanket – each in the finest wool she could buy (I think she went up to Winnipeg to buy it because wool of that quality was not available in any of the Fargo wool stores at the time.)

They were, to put it bluntly, absolutely utterly magnificent! The craftsmanship was undeniable – if she found an uneven stitch during the knitting, she would unravel the entire line or two of stitching and re-do it to get it right. The patterns were scaled to the size of the dolls – and they were absolutely perfect too.

This was Knitting Overkill on a massive scale. In addition to the craftsmanship, the artisanship was outstanding. But having Five of the identical outfits entered in the show was going to, as she put it, make it "damned hard for those old biddies" to come up with anything even remotely close.

And they didn't. She won, going away. Unlike the previous year, nobody had one negative word to say. Nor should they have. The exhibit was that good.

She came home that evening with what can only be described as a look of fierce satisfaction. "I sure showed those old biddies!" was the statement I remember best.

Yep – she surely did. And having made her sole statement, she never bothered to enter the event again. She had been there and done that – twice! Why go through the bother of doing it again?

There are those people who, as they age, fade gently into that good night. Not Mom. As she aged, she became even more judgmental of those whom she knew. I suspect some of that may have been the constant pain she had been experiencing from an undiagnosed ailment that plagued her right up until the end. Some of it may have been a dementia similar to the sort that took her own Mom years earlier.

She fought against going into a nursing home, but after moving down to Fergus Falls to live with my brother and his wife, he took her for a drive somewhere and wouldn't you know what happened.

So she ended up in the nursing home after all.

I was very ill when they family called, but as the eldest son there was no power on this earth that was going to keep me from that funeral. I took a red-eye to Minneapolis and drove to Grand Rapids to stay with a doctor friend while he pumped me full of appropriate medications so I could survive the drive to Fergus Falls.

At my friend's lake home, there is a tree where bald eagles have been roosting for over fifty years. On that March morning before I left for Fergus Falls, I found an eagle feather in the snow. At the funeral home, I tucked it into her jacket with a small Native American prayer to take her spirit and treat it kindly wherever her journey would take her.

She's buried in Ulen, Minnesota, not far from her own Mother.*

---

* It was my Mom's side of the family who were the Loyalists from Canada – but sometime in the '50s, my Mom's Mom moved from Sudbury, Ontario to live with us in Fargo. She later moved to a nursing home in Ulen, where she died and was buried.

Lots of memories of a complicated and interesting woman. Some great, some just OK and some that I wish I could forget – but can't. I cherish the good ones, as does my wife.

Those baby layettes she made over the years were mostly given away as hand-me-downs to someone else's children. They probably wore out and were thrown away, never recognized for the genuine folk art they were. I wonder where mine finally ended up? I have a picture of me wearing it as an infant.

I still have three hand-knit sweaters, all wool, one of alpaca. You can't buy anything that good anywhere. They all three have a label inside – "Made with Love, by Mom." I will never sell them or give them away. Wish I had someone to give them to who would treasure the memory as much as I.

We kept several of the cancer hats. My wife has given two of them away to others who have been going through their own throes with chemo. Each time they got the full story, with the instruction that they were to Pay It Forward by giving them away in turn.

So, Mom – we're doing the best we can to keep your contribution alive. You deserve that anyway. Rest in Peace – at long last.

You deserve it.

Je Regrette Nien!

I've never cared for the Acknowledgements page, where people are acknowledged before anyone really knows what they're being acknowledged for. So here's an Afterword, or perhaps an Afterthought, in which I mention maybe a dozen of the ones who Really stand out. There are more.

This was not an autobiography. It was merely a collection of anecdotes. There is so much more that Could be told, but I won't and never will. There's a reason why there's an Embarrassment gene in the human psyche – it's because some things are embarrassing. So don't ask, because I won't tell. There's too much anyway.

It's not meant to be a paean of praise to Fargo. As much as some Fargoans have enjoyed feeling smug about themselves, it'd be best not to get too carried away. It always was a small town, and like all small towns too many people knew the business of too many others. There was drama enough, a considerable amount of hanky-panky, some moments of stark betrayal and treachery and others of genuine human nobility.

Just like everywhere else.

I owe a debt to some of the people who played major roles in my experiences. We don't and can't repay such debts – those who were in the roles are mostly now either dead, or will be soon enough. The best we can hope for is the chance to Pay It Forward to others. I've tried to do that, and occasionally succeeded.

So a list – not complete, but pretty good, anyway. It's a group I'd enjoy inviting to dinner.

Vincent Dodge – Principal of Roosevelt Elementary School and later director of the choir at the First Methodist Church.

John Hildreth – The Eighth grade English teacher at Ben Franklin. I think he may well have figured me out. He certainly got me interested in English, when no other teacher had.

Pat (Geston) Hansen – The Eighth grade art teacher. She would give assignments, but mostly I drew pictures of airplanes. She became a friend and mentor, my freshman composition professor at NDSU and then, later still, my advanced composition professor. And after that, she may have given me the best advice I've ever received. I owe her more than most. I hold her memory more dear than any other.

Mary McKinney – The Ninth grade Latin teacher at Agassiz. When I transferred into her class, it soon became clear she'd done her research on me. She would assign one half of the class one half of the reading/translation lesson, and the others the other half. She held me responsible for both. I took it as a challenge and met it. Bless her heart.

Richard D. Olsen – Taught Western History at Fargo Central. A former Marine who wore a bow tie and was as good a teacher as I ever met. He found History to be occasionally as funny as I did.

Alice Jondahl – Taught the "accelerated" English class. I always had the feeling she really didn't like me. I learned later that she did – but she wasn't about to put up with any of my nonsense.

John Howard – Taught senior accelerated English. Got my first real taste of Shakespeare from him. I've been grateful ever since.

Phil Lestina – Taught Chemistry. Taught it well.

William Voth – Taught "accelerated" sophomore year Biology. Actually knew something about his subject other than what was in the book.

Sam Brekke – My best friend in high school. His dad, George, was the Fargo City Engineer. His mom, Marjorie, was just a delight. But Sam got into drugs and died twenty years or so ago. I wish he hadn't – I would have enjoyed becoming an old fart along with him. I miss him.

Steve Nelson – Another really good friend. His dad was the Cass County Engineer. I lost track of him several years after graduation, and have never been able to find him. Wish I could.

Jon Houtkooper – His dad ran Quality Bakery, on Broadway at the time. I recall the day Jon decided to take up smoking, sitting in the Taco Shop on University Drive. It eventually killed him.

Cheryl (Blenkush) Julien – She knows why.

E. James Ubbelohde – Taught Speech at NDSU. Just a fine teacher and a fine man.

Edwin Walker – Another fine Speech teacher. He got me started.

Donald F. Schwartz – Taught Communications Theory at NDSU. As bright and competent a researcher as I ever met.

Les Pavek – A good and kind man, with the misfortune of being the Dean of Students at NDSU while I was the newspaper editor there. He never could quite figure out how we could have an Understanding, but not an Agreement.

Laurel Loftsgard – The NDSU president. A native North Dakotan, but from the College of Agriculture, which made him suspect in the eyes of many of the faculty. A genuinely good guy, even if he bought into the football team thing more than was wise.

Franz Rathmann – Already an Emeritus professor when I was at NDSU. He actually had met the great pioneers in organic chemistry at Heidelberg, and had taught at the University of Saigon. He wrote long letters to me in Viet Nam full of chemical reaction equations and little else. My friends there thought that very strange!

Maria Prausnitz – My piano teacher at the Concordia Conservatory of Music. Her family fled Germany prior to Hitler. A damned fine piano teacher!

Herschel Laschkowitz – Fargo mayor for about a millennium (his 1954-74 term in office is still the longest on record). Friend of my Dad's. I was the first person to interview him for my school newspaper when he first won election. I don't know that anybody was really His friend, but I considered him a friend of mine.

Torfin Teigen – A true Child of Fargo. To those who knew him, it's obvious why he's mentioned. (To those who didn't, it won't matter.) If you're curious, ask around. He was sui generis – to a fault. A genuine character – probably quite mad. But also quite harmless. He was always showing up around town, especially at official events that caught his eye, constantly going to run for some office, and was generally considered to be the Village Character. He'd call up a talk radio program on WDAY – Viewpoint, then hosted by Bob Aronson (whom some of the locals considered to be a close cousin of Karl Marx) – and do some rant for whatever his time period was, then he'd leave. He'd show up in the offices of elected officials with various cockamamie writings and rantings about this or that official policy thing.

One time I recall he showed up in some congresscritter's office saying that he'd just bought a train ticket to DC because he was going to be appointed Secretary of Agriculture. He was serious about that, and some of the locals sort of took charge of him and got him off of that.

But personally, he was harmless. He didn't get angry, didn't threaten to shoot anyone, and was more or less just a really interesting fellow. I suspect many found him somewhat embarrassing, but my own view was always that he was simply monitoring different frequencies than everyone else was, and since he didn't do or try to do anyone any harm, it was best just to tolerate him.

I mention him – really – just because I think he Should be mentioned. No one else is ever likely to, and a local character like that deserves to have some hysterical/historical mention somewhere. It'd be a real shame of all record of his name disappeared entirely from folks' ken.

But don't make too much of him. The common reaction to his antics would be "Oh – that's just Teigen," with a smile, and folks would get on with their own lives

There are others who deserve acknowledgement, but this is already too much like an Academy Awards speech. I have been greatly privileged to know such people and have such friends. I am whoever I am in no small part because of them. I am grateful. They may or may not share that.

Socrates once said, "The unexamined life is not worth living." (He was on trial for heresy at the time, and there are too many parallels for me to follow that idea to its inevitable conclusion.) I am now 70. That's about twice as long as my Dad lived, and easily three times longer than I believed I would live when I was in Viet Nam. I figure at this point, I have had my allotted three score and ten, and after this it's anyone's guess what happens.

So an examination is fully in order. The complete diagnosis can wait till later.

When I told a few friends about this project, several suggested that I use as a theme the Frank Sinatra ballad, "I Did It My Way."

On reflection, No – neither a good idea, nor applicable. I did Not do it all my way. I did sometimes, but a lot of time I was merely caught up in events, and attempted to find a way through them in a rational fashion. So this is Not an epistle of praise for a fiercely independent life. It wasn't. Few ever are.

On a couple of occasions while in Viet Nam, I promised myself that whatever else might happen to me, if I got out of the immediate situation I would lead an Interesting life above all else. Life is either a daring adventure, or it is nothing at all. Given a choice, I've gone with the adventure, and not the safer path.

But there is a Frank Sinatra ballad that does perhaps apply.

And now the days grow short
I'm in the autumn of my years
And now I think of my life
As vintage wine
From fine old kegs.
From the brim to the dregs
It pours sweet and clear
It was a very good year

So thank you, Fargo, for being a major part of all those memories and formative events. I am who I am because of you and the people who lived there. I am by no means smug about that. I never became Rich and Famous. I never became the Great Scientist I had intended to be, until war took that out of me. But it has been Interesting – that above all.

I continue to do Useful Political Work, even while not Being A Politician. I still suck up to no one, seek no interest's support or favor, and am still able to do what I consider to be The Right Thing in all of that.

Those are values I learned while in Fargo, I suspect.

I have learned, over the years, that there is no End of good things one can get done, provided one is willing to either share or let someone else take credit for the outcomes.

That's another value I learned in Fargo, I suspect.

I have always never really quite trusted praise. When it's effusive, it always Feels to me as though someone has their own agenda rather than mine. Am I proud of what I do – yes,

289

decidedly. I have an ego sufficient to believe that when I do some good thing, I can take a great deal of personal pride in it. But it's mostly internal – not something I choose to make a big deal out of publicly.

That, too, is a value I learned while in Fargo.

Though sometimes, public attention is unavoidable – as with the strange map. I was astonished at how that went worldwide, but deliberately moved not to profit from it, as one fellow from Europe wanted me to, by licensing the rights to make T-shirts of it. The thing itself, if done well, is sufficient.

And that too is value I undoubtedly learned in Fargo.

I am also largely indifferent to most criticism. While not bloody-minded or bullheaded, I go to considerable lengths to fully consider and take the Long View of what I do and why.

And I bet you know where I was when I became that way.

As one Very good friend of mine in graduate school once said, I am *sui generis* to a fault.

Perhaps not as much as Torfin Teigen. But again, there's no denying that much, if not most, of who I am, came to fullness in Fargo. And Fargo is, undeniably, more than just a little *sui generis* itself.

As that great (I would like to say Unsung, but really can't in this case) American philosopher, Ricky Nelson, wrote in his great song, *Garden Party*: "You see you can't please everyone, so you've got to please yourself."

*   *   *

One final thought:

You have your own stories – perhaps even some about Being Fargo and undoubtedly some about other places and people and events. History isn't just about the Big Deal events that get into newspapers. It is, or should be, as much about how regular people Lived, and Loved (that maybe especially) and found a way to deal with the Ups and Downs that Life throws at them.

Tell your stories. Share them with family and friends – especially the friends who shared the experiences with you. Write them down and pass them on. If that's too difficult, record them somehow. They're important.

So are you.

Be well.

Don Homuth lived in Fargo from 1953 - 1980. He graduated from Fargo Central High School (1962) and NDSU (1970). While in Fargo, he was active in the community. He now lives on a small farm in Oregon with his wife of 25 years, Kathy Cegla, where he still tells stories.

CPSIA information can be obtained
at www.ICGtesting.com
Printed in the USA
FSOW02n0551300715
9388FS